EXPLORING
1·2·3
JOHN

EXPLORING 1·2·3 JOHN

JERRY VINES

LOIZEAUX BROTHERS

Neptune, New Jersey

EXPLORING 1, 2, 3 JOHN
©1989 Jerry Vines. All rights reserved.

Published by Loizeaux Brothers, Inc., a nonprofit
organization devoted to Lord's work and to the spread of
his truth.

Portions of the commentary on John's first epistle
appeared originally in a book by Dr. Vines entitled
Family Fellowship.

Printed in the United States of America.

ISBN 0-87213-894-1

Foreword   7
Preface   9

I JOHN

   1. It's Real   13
   2. Fellowship with God   26
   3. What to do with Our Sins   36
   4. Old, Yet New   47
   5. Growing Up   58
   6. Worldliness   69
   7. Those Who Go Away   80
   8. How Do You Want to Meet Him?   92
   9. It's Out of This World   101
  10. Sinless Perfection   111
  11. Satan Is Alive but Not Well   120
  12. Where Love Cannot Be   131
  13. The Cure for an Accusing Heart   141
  14. Truth and Error   149
  15. Love Is the Theme   158
  16. Perfect Love   167
  17. Birthmarks of a Believer   175
  18. The Witness of the Spirit   186
  19. Boldness in Prayer   195
  20. Sin unto Death   204
  21. A Trinity of Certainty   213

2 JOHN

  22. Love in the Truth   222

3 JOHN

  23. Living the Truth   232

Conclusion   241

Foreword

I T IS WITH GREAT DELIGHT THAT I PEN THE FOREWORD TO THIS DELIGHT-
ful and pertinent volume. Jerry Vines is an able expositor of
the word of God. Here, with warm and vital application, he
presents the truths found in the first epistle of John.

The messages come from the heart of a prophet. Dr. Vines
preaches as he writes, and vice versa. This book burns with
Bible fire that leaps up from the pages and into the heart.

Jerry Vines has so outlined and illustrated this study that one
need not wade through wasted words nor wonder at the ideas
presented. Bible teachers will be grateful for the author's clear,
vigorous style. Lay persons will be blessed by the devotional
reading contained here. Also, I have no doubt but that preachers of the gospel will find valuable aid in the presentation of the
truths contained here.

This is the kind of book one wishes to pass on to a friend after
having read it. I commend it with a whole heart.

ADRIAN ROGERS
Pastor, Bellevue Baptist Church
Memphis, Tennessee

Preface

THE TITLE I ORIGINALLY GAVE TO THIS SERIES OF SERMONS, "FAMILY Fellowship," was taken from the twofold emphasis of 1 John. In the first two chapters the book speaks of being in fellowship with God. The last three chapters deal with being in the family of God. These messages were preached on Sunday evenings as I began fellowship with a new family of God's people, Dauphin Way Baptist Church in Mobile, Alabama. I found those dear people to be just that—a wonderful, happy family. Our fellowship with one another and the Lord Jesus was increasingly sweet. I hope you can sense the joy I felt as I shared the things the Lord opened to me in 1 John.

I am no scholar. I am simply a Bible-believing preacher who tries to preach the word to his people. I have not tried to be profound; in the heat of delivery the finer points of style are sometimes overlooked. Neither am I original. I have relied heavily on the works of others. But I have prayed the material into my heart and delivered it as the Lord has led me. I milk a lot of cows, but I try to make my own butter.

May the Lord use these messages to guide you the reader into a deeper experience of family fellowship.

1 JOHN

1

It's Real
1 John 1:1–4

I. THE CHRIST OF REALITY
  A. Eternally
  B. Historically
  C. Experientially
II. THE CHRIST OF RELATIONSHIP
  A. A Family
  B. The Father
III. THE CHRIST OF REJOICING
  A. Salvation
  B. Scriptures
  C. Soulwinning

THE LORD JESUS LOVED ALL OF HIS DISCIPLES, BUT SEVERAL OF THEM HAD greater capacity to respond to his love than others. Because of that, they came to be known as his inner circle. Among them, a man named John is known as the beloved disciple. He was a fisherman who met the Lord at the beginning of his ministry, and from that time until the resurrection and ascension he was very close to the Lord.

This John, the beloved disciple, is the author of five of the New Testament books. John gave us the gospel of John, 1 John, 2 John, 3 John, and the final book of the Bible, Revelation. These five books are in three main groups. First is the gospel, which has to do with our past and deals with the theme of salvation. The three epistles have to do with our present and deal with the theme of sanctification or daily growth in the Christian life. The last book, Revelation, points to the future, that glorious time when we shall see him.

It is characteristic of John in his writings to put a key either at the front or back door of the book, which will unlock its meaning. For instance, in the book of Revelation the key is hanging at the front. In verse 19 of the first chapter, John was told by the Lord, "Write the things which thou hast seen, and the things which are, and the things which shall be hereafter." That simple outline is the key to understanding the Revelation. In his gospel the key is at the end: "These are written, that ye might believe that Jesus is the Christ, the Son of God; and that believing ye might have life through his name" (John 20:31). The gospel of John was written so that people might come to know the Lord. If you know someone who is not a Christian, the best thing you can do for them is put into their hands a copy of the gospel of John, since John says that the book was written for the specific purpose of helping people come to believe that Jesus is the Christ and thus have eternal life.

In 1 John four keys unlock the meaning of the book, all identified by the phrase, "These things I write." One key is at the back door, near the end of the book. There John says this: "These things have I written unto you that believe on the name of the Son of God . . ." (1 John 5:13). There we see a difference between 1 John and the gospel of John. In his gospel, John said, "I am writing that ye may believe." In this little epistle he says, "I am writing to those of you who do believe that Jesus is the Son of God." Why is John writing to believers? "That ye may know that ye have eternal life, and that ye may believe on the name of the Son of God." John is saying, "I am writing this book to Christians so they can know they have eternal life." This word *know* should be circled in your Bible; it is the key word in 1 John. In these chapters John says "we know" over thirty times. Some people say, "Well, you cannot really know anything. You cannot really know you are going to heaven when you die." Yet John says, "I am writing these things so you may know that you have eternal life."

The first key, the first purpose of the book of 1 John, is to provide assurance for the child of God. Are you sure of your salvation? If I did not know beyond the shadow of a doubt that Jesus

Christ is my personal Savior I would not finish reading this chapter until I had that assurance.

People lack assurance of salvation for one of two reasons. They lack assurance because they have no basis for assurance. A person who has never been truly born again cannot be sure that he or she is a child of God. Or, they may lack assurance because they do not know the word of God; they do not know the basis of assurance. We can know we are saved because God has told us so in his word. So the first key to the book is this: It is written to provide assurance to the child of God.

The second key is found in 1 John 2:26. "These things have I written unto you concerning them that seduce you." John's second purpose is to protect the saints (Christians) against those who would lead them astray.

There are many false doctrines going around in our land today. There are many forms of doctrinal departure from the word of God and many false teachers whose purpose is to seduce the child of God. So we have a specific book in the Bible written to protect us against those who would lead us into error.

The third key is found in 1 John 2:1. "My little children, these things write I unto you, that ye sin not." He is writing in order to prevent sin. Nowhere does the Bible tell us that a child of God will not sin. Some people get the idea, "Well, if I become a Christian, that means I am not going to sin any more. I cannot stop sinning. Therefore I will not become a Christian." The Bible nowhere says that a Christian is sinless, but it does teach that a child of God ought to sin less. Day by day we ought to grow in grace, and sin less today than we did yesterday. John says, "I am writing you this book so that you will not sin."

The fourth key, the fourth reason for writing the book, is found in 1 John 1:4. "And these things write we unto you, that your joy may be full." John is writing to promote joy in the heart of the child of God.

Do you have joy today? I mean, are you happy in the Lord? Do you really know Christ as your Savior? Do you really enjoy being a Christian? It seems to me that some people have just enough religion to make them miserable. It is like a headache. You cannot stand it, yet you cannot get rid of your head. Some people want just enough religion to get them to church occasionally, yet not enough to give them real joy in their heart. John says, "I am writing to you that your joy may be full."

After that brief introduction, let us look at John's opening verses. He gives no words of introduction, no word of greeting to anyone. This is for all of God's people everywhere. John begins with the Lord Jesus Christ, "the Word of life" (1 John 1:1). Only John in the New Testament identifies the Lord Jesus as the "Word." In John 1:1 scripture says, "In the beginning was the Word." In Revelation 19:12–13 we are told, "And he had a name . . . and his name is called The Word of God." In his epistle, John identifies Jesus by this phrase, "the Word of life."

What is the purpose of a word? You and I communicate with one another by using words. I speak words in the pulpit and thereby I communicate what is in my mind. John is saying that Jesus Christ is God's communication to us. Jesus is the noun of God, the verb of God, the adjective of God. Jesus articulates God. When you look at Jesus Christ you see the love of God. When you look at Jesus you see the holiness of God. When you listen to Jesus you are listening to God. So John begins with the Lord Jesus Christ and goes on to tell us three truths about him in these verses.

I. THE CHRIST OF REALITY

Christ is real. Here we need to grasp some of the background. John was writing about the reality of Jesus in order to counteract a heresy current in New Testament days. It was the heresy known as Gnosticism, which comes from the Greek word *gnosis* (meaning "to know"). The Gnostics believed that all matter was evil and therefore they could not believe that Jesus had an actual, physical, material body. They denied his humanity. They said that Jesus did not actually live, that he merely appeared to live, that Jesus was a phantom. Others said that Jesus was a human being and that the divine Christ came upon him at his baptism and departed at his crucifixion.

The thrust of the matter was that they did not believe in the incarnation, the literal coming into human existence of the Lord Jesus Christ. What John is doing is immediately attacking the heretics who denied Jesus' humanity. He is saying, "This Jesus I am talking about is real. He actually exists."

In these opening two verses he speaks of Christ's threefold reality.

A. Eternally

First, Christ is real eternally. Here I am going to discuss more than I fully understand. Do you know people who say, "I don't accept anything I don't understand." Well, I accept a lot of things I don't understand. For example, I don't understand electricity. They say that one electron touches another electron and all of that, but I don't know why it happens to go one way instead of the other way. I don't understand electricity, but I accept it and I don't put my thumb in a light bulb socket. So we are going to jump into the eternal realm for a moment. John begins by saying, "That which was from the beginning. . . ." Now if you can understand that, I'd like you to explain it to me.

In fact, three main beginnings are mentioned in scripture. The first one is obvious. In Genesis 1:1 we are told about the beginning of creation. "In the beginning God created the heaven and the earth." In Mark 1:1 we are told about another beginning, "The beginning of the gospel of Jesus Christ, the Son of God . . . ." Here is a third beginning: "That which was from the beginning. . . ." What John is saying is, "From the moment of creation Jesus Christ existed." He is talking about the pre-existence of Jesus. In John 1:1 he goes a little further. He begins his gospel by saying, "In the beginning," not "from the beginning," but "In the beginning was the Word." Do you see the difference? In 1 John 1:1 it is "from the beginning." Jesus Christ has existed from the beginning of all things but, in his gospel, John goes back farther and says, "Why, before all creation came into existence, Christ was." He is declaring that Jesus is God. Scripture says, "In the beginning was the Word, and the Word was with God, and the Word was God." Jesus Christ is coexistent, coeternal, coequal with God, the Father. Jesus said, "He that hath seen me hath seen God" (see John 12:45). In Hebrews 13:8 we read, "Jesus Christ the same yesterday, and today, and for ever."

18

B. Historically

Second, John is saying that Christ is real historically. At this point we dip into time and touch history: "For the life was manifested . . ." (1 John 1:2). The word *manifested* means "to appear" or "to be made visible." The eternal Christ who existed in eternity with the Father, the invisible Christ, was born, became visible, and lived and moved on this earth. That is what Paul called a *mystery*: "Great is the mystery of godliness: God was manifest in the flesh" (1 Timothy 3:16). John 1:14 puts it this way: "And the Word was made flesh, and dwelt among us."

Do you see what John is trying to convey? Do you see the import of this truth? They did not have television or tape recorders, but if they had, you could have taped the voice of the Lord Jesus; you could have taken his picture; you could have filmed the experiences of his life. He was a flesh-and-blood person. Yes, he was more than a mere man, but he was a man. That is what John is trying to say. If Jesus was real, if he actually lived, he could have been perceived by the senses. That is what John says in verse 1, and he appeals to three of the senses that identify a person as a real person.

First, underline the word *heard*. John is saying, "We heard it."

I think John probably heard Jesus say more words than any other disciple. He was with him from the beginning. In the inner circle he heard the voice of Jesus. Have you ever wondered how Jesus' voice sounded? I would like to have heard the voice of Jesus. Wouldn't you like to have heard how Jesus said some of the things he said? John says, "I heard him." In fact, the tense of the verb here means an action that began in times past with the effect that it still continues. John is saying, "This Jesus is real; I actually heard his words, and they are still ringing in my ears."

Second, underline the word *seen*. John is saying, "I saw him. I actually saw Jesus with my eyes."

You and I have never seen Jesus with our physical eyes, but John did. This is the thing that authenticates the New Testament. Jesus Christ was seen by eyewitnesses.

Some people say, "Well, they had an hallucination." John takes care of that with the next statement. "We have seen with our eyes, . . . we have looked upon." The word *look* is the word from which we get the word *theater,* and it means more than just a glimpse. It means an intense gaze. It is the idea of looking with examination. It is the idea of looking and understanding and perceiving what you are seeing. John declares, "We looked upon him, we examined him. It was no hallucination. It was no passing glance. It was an intense gaze. We really saw the Lord Jesus Christ."

Third, underline the word *handled.* He says, "We handled him," and what he means is "We touched him." Jesus had a real physical body. Now I have said on occasion that I believe Jesus weighed 180 pounds and was six feet tall. Folks look at me and say, "That isn't in the Bible." No, it isn't, but the point I am trying to make is this: He did weigh something and he did have some kind of physical stature.

In Luke 24 Jesus is resurrected, comes to his disciples, yet he had a body. He had a body unlike the body you and I have now, but one of these days we are going to have a body like the one he has now. I don't understand that kind of body, one able to go through closed doors. You say, "That is a miracle." Why, of course, Jesus is a miracle.

I do not have trouble with miracles. When I see the miracles that modern science is able to perform, I have no trouble in believing the miracle that God was manifest in the flesh and walked among us, that he actually and literally existed on earth. After his resurrection he appeared to his disciples and said, "Behold my hands and my feet, that it is I myself" (Luke 24:39). "Handle me and see; for a spirit hath not flesh and bones, as ye see me have."

John is saying, "I heard him with my ears, I saw him with my eyes, I touched him with my hands." Jesus Christ is real historically.

C. Experientially

This Christ of reality is real experientially. Christianity is a personal experience with the Lord Jesus Christ. You have never seen Jesus physically. That is true, but John moved from physical nearness with Jesus to spiritual nearness to Jesus. The Bible teaches that we know him by faith. Faith becomes the hands, the eyes, the ears of the soul. By faith we apprehend the Lord Jesus Christ, and he becomes real in our personal experience.

Christianity is not knowing Christ in a historical sense; it is knowing Jesus Christ in a personal experience. This is the difference between church membership and salvation. Church members may know about Jesus, but born-again believers know Jesus as their own personal Savior. I know about a lot of people, but I do not know them. I know about Pope John Paul, but I have never met him. I cannot say I am personally acquainted with him. It is not enough to know about Jesus. We must know Jesus Christ in a personal way. Scripture says, "If thou shalt confess with thy mouth the Lord Jesus, and shalt believe in thine heart that God hath raised him from the dead, thou shalt be saved" (Romans 10:9). So the first thing John says about Jesus is this: "He is real, the Christ of reality." We are talking about real things. We are talking about a real Jesus.

II. THE CHRIST OF RELATIONSHIP

John also talks about the Christ of relationship (1 John 1:3). The word *fellowship* is one of the greatest words in the Bible. The Greek word *koinonia* means "to have in common," to "share something together." It is a distinctly Christian word.

The lost world has taken the word and applied it to many things. People talk about a fellowship at their club or at a party, but in the New Testament sense of the word, the only people who experience fellowship are those who have received Jesus Christ and who know him in reality. Fellowship means to share together, to enjoy the same things together.

The fellowship John talks to us about is a twofold relationship. It is first of all horizontal, fellowship with one another; it is also vertical, fellowship with God the Father.

A. A Family

First we have fellowship with a family. John says, "I want you to have fellowship with us." That is horizontal, you and me. "I want us to have fellowship together."

Some teach that God is the Father of everybody and we are all brothers and sisters. That sounds good, but the problem is, it just is not so. There are two families in this world. Jesus said, "Ye are of your father the devil." There is the family of the devil and the family of God. The only way we get into the family of God is through a new-birth experience. We got into the other family when we were born physically. Our natural, physical birth brought us into the family of Adam, and the only way we get into the family of God is to be born into it. We do not get baptized into it. We do not join a church and get our name on the roll and get in it that way. We have to be born into the family of God.

When we are born into God's family we become part of the greatest fellowship in all the world. Galatians 2:9 says the believers extended to Paul and Barnabas the right hand of fellowship. When a person joins our church we shake her or his hand. We say, "Welcome to the fellowship," the most meaningful fellowship on earth.

This poor lost world knows nothing of fellowship. If you want to be with a bunch of deadbeats, if you want to be bored to death, get in some worldly crowd going to cocktail parties and bridge parties and all of that. They are trying to impress one another, outdo one another, and they are bored to tears. But if you want to have fun, if you really want to live, get into fellowship with a group of wide-awake, on-fire, born-again children of God.

Christians enjoy the things of God. Philippians 2:1 talks about the "fellowship of the Spirit." You cannot touch it, you can hardly describe it, but it is there. Philippians 1:5 talks about "your fellowship in the gospel." We enjoy the things of the gospel together.

Acts 2:42 talks about believers after the day of Pentecost and says, "They continued stedfastly in the apostles' doctrine and fellowship, and in breaking of bread, and in prayers." They were enjoying studying the Bible, partaking of the Lord's supper, witnessing for Jesus Christ. They had something in common.

Every child of God ought to take 2 Corinthians 6:14 seriously. If young people will put this verse in their heart and will follow it, it will save them a lot of trouble out there in the future. "Be ye not unequally yoked together with unbelievers." A saved, born-again young person has no business marrying a lost young person. This is why. "For what fellowship hath righteousness with unrighteousness? and what communion hath light with darkness?" If a young woman marries an unbeliever, she is out of the will of God. How can she possibly expect their home to be what it ought to be? And vice versa. If you marry someone lost, perhaps a skeptic who makes fun of Jesus, you may have a lifetime of grief. God's people must not have fellowship with lost people. Friendship, yes, but not fellowship. You do not share the same things. Young people, if you cannot pray on a date, you ought not to have that date. If you cannot get that girl or boy to church, you ought to quit going with that person. If he or she does not have respect for your Jesus, just mark him or her off your list. You do not need that date. In his own time, God will give you a good marriage partner.

One night I was preaching in a revival meeting and I said, "You ought to pray for a mate; pray that God will give you the right wife or husband." The next night some of the young girls came up and said, "We had a prayer meeting last night." I said, "Great! Praying for the revival?" They said, "No, praying for a husband!" That is all right. We are in fellowship with a family. We enjoy the things of God together.

B. The Father

Second, there is also a vertical fellowship. John says, "We want you to have fellowship with the Father." Fellowship with the family is great, but here we are, Adam-creatures, in comparison to the great creator, God. Yet the God of this universe has said, "I want to have fellowship with you."

How do you have fellowship with God? It is simple. You have fellowship with God through the Bible and prayer. You read the Bible; God talks to you. You pray; you talk to God. That is a dialogue. The greatest experience that can come to any person in this world is through the new-birth experience, being brought into the family of God and thereby into fellowship with God. The Christ we preach is the Christ of relationship.

III. THE CHRIST OF REJOICING

Our Christ is the Christ of rejoicing. John said, "I want your joy to be full" (1 John 1:4). The word *full* means "to be filled full."

I want you to have total joy, not one-fourth full, not one-half full, I want it full!

This is another word peculiar to the Christian faith. Lost persons do not have joy. The Bible does say that lost persons can have pleasure. Some people are living in sin and rather enjoying it. The Bible tells us of the pleasures of sin, but they are for a season. Every trinket this world has to offer loses its glitter.

Look at the faces of people; there is no joy. Why, our generation has more to offer, more entertainments, more amusements, than any generation has ever had, yet look at the loneliness in the eyes of the people you see, the worried expression on their face. Look at the desire so evident in them for something they have not found.

You do not find joy in this world. Psalm 16:11 says, "In thy presence is fulness of joy." If you want joy, come to Jesus. It is a spiritual commodity that cannot be purchased in the stores of this world. It can be granted only at the throne of God. Do you have joy? For the Christian there is joy in several places. I will mention just a few.

A. Salvation

There is joy in salvation. Isaiah 12:3 says, "Therefore with joy shall ye draw water out of the wells of salvation." It is a joy to be a Christian. The most joyous truth in my heart is to know that Jesus Christ is my personal Savior, that my home is in heaven, and that I have a reason to be living.

I have a book, *Deeper Experiences of Famous Christians*, that has a story about Billy Bray, one of God's quaint vessels. He would offend some Christians today, but he had a real experience of salvation and he did not know what to do except express himself. They made fun of Billy Bray and laughed at him. "Why, Billy Bray, you are so happy, so joyous, all the time. Suppose you discovered that you are not saved at all, you are really not a child of God, and suppose when you die you go to hell?" Billy Bray said, "Well, I suppose if I die and I discover that I am not a Christian and I go to hell, Jesus has been so real and so wonderful and precious to me in life I will just have to shout all the way to hell. When I get down to hell I will have to run up and down the streets of hell shouting 'Hallelujah, praise the Lord.' The devil will come over to me and say, 'Billy Bray, we cannot stand that down here; we cannot put up with that. We will just have to send you to heaven.'" That is the joy of salvation.

B. Scriptures

The Christian draws joy from the scriptures. Jeremiah 15:16 can start you on a pilgrimage to joy. If you will do what it says there, you will have a life running over with joy. "Thy words were found, and I did eat them." Listen to what the prophet is saying: "The Bible is just like a good meal to me."

Do you feel that way about your Bible? Can you say, "Your word, Lord, is like a good meal. Your word brought joy and rejoicing to my heart." Do you know why most Christians don't have much joy? It is because they don't study the Bible; they don't even read the Bible. Bible-reading Christians are like children on Christmas morning who open up their presents, and every box gets better and better and better, and they are running over with exuberance and joy. That is the way it is when Christians daily study the Bible and uncover these treasures. They have a joyful time.

Would you start doing that? Could I get you to start in the morning and open up your New Testament and read a chapter, and then do that again the next morning and the next morning until you have gone through the whole New Testament? If I can get you to do that, at the end of 260 days you will come back to me and say, "I have discovered more joy than I have ever known in all my life."

C. Soulwinning

There is joy in soulwinning. Some of the early manuscripts of 1 John translate "our joy" instead of "your joy." Either way, there is a wonderful truth, but if it is "our joy," John is saying, "The greatest joy that could come to me would be for you to come to know my Jesus." In 1 Thessalonians 2:20 Paul says, "For ye are our glory and joy." He is saying, "It is a joy to win people to faith in the Lord Jesus Christ."

A little boy came up outside a rescue mission, put his nose and face up against a window, and looked in where they were having a sumptuous meal. He was so hungry. The man in charge saw him, went out and got him, and brought him inside. He sat him down to the meal and expected him to start eating. Instead, the child began to cry. The man said, "Son, what is the matter with you?" The boy replied, "Mister, this meal looks real good, but I have a buddy across the street and he is hungry too. I can't be happy until he is eating what I eat."

Do you know anybody who needs Jesus? Although there is joy in knowing the Lord yourself, we feel pain for those who do not know him. Samuel Rutherford said about his members at Anwoth, "Oh, if one soul in Anwoth meet me at God's right hand, my heaven shall be two heavens in Immanuel Land."

The late Dr. Roland Q. Leavell, president of New Orleans Baptist Theological Seminary, told this story shortly before he died. He was preaching in a meeting in Washington, D.C., and after the service a young woman came up to him. She said, "Dr. Leavell, when I was nine years old, on a hot Monday afternoon in a little Mississippi town, you came to my house and introduced me to Jesus. I let him come into my heart. I have not always been what I should have been, but since that time I have tried to live as near to Jesus as I know how to live." Dr. Leavell said to her, "Will you do something for me?" She said, "Yes, sir, if I can." He said, "When we get to heaven, would you permit me to take you by the hand and lead you to the throne of King Jesus? And will you tell him what you have just told me? If you will, it will be heaven enough for me."

"These things write we unto you, that our joy may be full."

2

Fellowship with God
1 John 1:5–7

I. THE BASIS OF THIS FELLOWSHIP
  A. Positively
  B. Negatively
II. THE BREAKING OF THIS FELLOWSHIP
  A. Profession
  B. Practice
  C. Prevarication
III. THE BLESSING OF THIS FELLOWSHIP
  A. Walking with God
  B. Washed in the Blood

TWO RELATIONSHIPS WITH GOD ARE CONSIDERED IN 1 JOHN. ONE IS THE relationship of sonship, which has to do with being in the family of God. John 1:12 says, "But as many as received him, to them gave he power to become the sons of God, even to them that believe on his name." When you come to chapters 3, 4, and 5 in 1 John, you will notice that frequently John talks about being sons of God, children of God, and about being born of God. This is the relationship that comes about through the new-birth experience. We are born into the family of God and thus have sonship. This relationship is an eternal relationship and can never be broken. You can give yourself several tests as you study 1 John to help determine whether or not you have sonship, whether or not you are in the family of God.

The second relationship is the matter of fellowship. All Christians have sonship; they are in the family of God. It is also possible for all Christians to have fellowship with and be in the favor of God. There is a difference between sonship, or being in God's family, and fellowship, or being in the favor of God. It is possible for our fellowship with God to be broken, as we shall see in the next chapter. But here the theme is "fellowship with God," indeed a lofty one. Who can imagine the ramifications of a human being having fellowship with God? To think that God would invite us to have fellowship with him, walk with him, get acquainted with him!

I. THE BASIS OF THIS FELLOWSHIP

"This then is the message which we have heard of him, and declare unto you, that God is light, and in him is no darkness at all" (1 John 1:5). If we are going to have fellowship with God, we must understand the basis of that fellowship, the terms by which God agrees to have fellowship with humankind. The basic premise is this simple statement: "God is light." This is the basis of our fellowship. Later on we have another statement about God: "For God is love" (1 John 4:8). This is the basis of our sonship. It is possible for us to be sons of God because God is love. But it is possible for us to have fellowship with God because God is light. That is the fundamental premise.

A. Positively

Our fellowship with God is stated in a twofold manner. John presents the premise positively and says, God is light. John does not say, God has a light or God is a light. God in his nature is light; God's essence, his being, is light. The psalmist declares, "The Lord is my light and my salvation" (Psalm 27:1). In 1 Timothy 6:16 we are told that God dwells in unapproachable light.

When John says that God is light, he has in mind several truths. First, he is speaking physically of the glory of God. As you study the Bible you will notice that every time God comes on the scene there is light. For instance, in Genesis 1 we are told that darkness was on the face of the deep. Then God said, Let there be light, and there was light. When God came down in the tabernacle, he came in the shekinah glory cloud of light. That is why I like to have plenty of light in church. I do not like to go into buildings where you can hardly see. I want plenty of light, because we are coming to visit the God of light. Physically, light represents the glory of God.

Intellectually, to say that God is light represents the knowledge of God. The Bible declares that God has all knowledge. God knows everything; there is nothing we can teach God; there is nothing God can learn because God knows everything. God sees us and knows us. He knows where we have been and where we are going.

Morally, to say that God is light represents the holiness of God. This is the primary reference here. John is making a statement about the character of God. He is saying that God is absolutely holy. God is totally moral; nothing whatsoever in God is wrong. James 1:13 declares that God cannot be tempted with evil, nor does he tempt any one.

B. Negatively

The premise is also stated negatively. John continues by saying that there is no darkness at all in God. In the Greek text it is a double negative. There is not no darkness in God. That is not good English, but it is good theology. There is no imperfection whatsoever in God. There is no spot on the character of God, no blemish on the being of God, not one shadow of suspicion. The Bible calls God the "Father of lights, with whom is no variableness [that is, he does not change], neither shadow of turning" (James 1:17).

It is important for us to think right thoughts about the character and personality of God. Our concept of God will ultimately determine the kind of life we live. If we have a low concept of God, then we will live a low life. If we have a high concept of God, we will be challenged to live a high and noble life. The Bible says, "O Lord God of Israel, thou art righteous" (Ezra 9:15). Isaiah heard the seraphim declare, "Holy, holy, holy, is the Lord of hosts" (Isaiah 6:3). We need to learn to appreciate the holiness of God. When we come to worship God, we ought to approach him in an attitude of reverence and respect. We also ought to come with an attitude of expectancy and response in our heart.

Because God is holy, he cannot and will not tolerate sin. Scripture says, "Thou art of purer eyes than to behold evil, and canst not look on iniquity" (Habakkuk 1:13). So it is necessary that we walk in the light if we are going to have fellowship with God.

II. The Breaking of This Fellowship

We have already noted that our sonship with God can never be broken. If a child is born into your family, it is your child eternally. It is possible, however, for your child to get out of your favor. Things can enter in that will come between you and the child, and your fellowship with one another will be broken. Your child may even break your heart, but he or she cannot break the parent-child relationship. This is what John is talking about in verse 6. Let us consider three things.

A. Profession

First, we look at our profession. "If we say that we have fellowship with him . . ." (1 John 1:6). Here is a person who says, "I am walking with God. I am in fellowship with God." That is a tremendous claim, isn't it? If I should ask if you are in fellowship with God, you would probably say yes. You would make a profession that you are in fellowship with God. You are declaring that you share things with God, that you have things in common with God. You are saying, "I have come from darkness into light."

The Bible says many things about darkness. It says that this world is in darkness; the whole world lies in darkness. In our natural condition, we human beings are in the power of darkness. However, the Bible says, "[God] hath delivered us from the power of darkness, and hath translated us into the kingdom of his dear Son" (Colossians 1:13). In 1 Peter 2:9 the Bible says that God has called us out of darkness and has placed us in his marvelous light. When you say you are in fellowship with God, you are saying, "I have stepped out of darkness and into the light."

You are also saying, "I am walking in the light." In verse 6,

John talks about walking in darkness, and in verse 7 in contrast he talks about walking in the light. The person who says, "I have fellowship with God," is saying, "I am walking in the light." The Bible says, "For ye were sometimes darkness, but now are ye light in the Lord: walk as children of light" (Ephesians 5:8).

B. Practice

Second, we see the practice. "If we say that we have fellowship with him, and walk in darkness . . . " (1 John 1:6). There is a great deal of difference between profession and practice. It is one thing to claim something; it is another thing for it to be true. Not every one who says he or she is a Christian *is* a Christian. Jesus says, "Not every one that saith unto me, Lord, Lord, shall enter into the kingdom of heaven" (Matthew 7:21). Words will not get anyone into heaven. Just because you say you are going to heaven does not mean you are. Professing Christ as your Savior does not mean that you possess Jesus Christ in your heart. Rather, are you actually walking with God? In fact, many people profess more than they practice. Some are long on lip, but short on life. Some can quote the Bible by the yard, yet they live it by the inch.

What does it mean to walk in darkness? According to the way John uses the idea here, it means to walk in sin and disobedience. It means to practice things that are contrary to the holiness and light of God.

John was attacking a heresy that was rampant in his day. Some people were saying that it was possible to be in fellowship with God and to be in sin at the same time.

I once talked with a man who said, "I know I don't talk as I ought to talk; I know I say some things I ought not to say, but it is not really me talking. I really don't mean it with my heart." That is the kind of thing John is dealing with here. Many people are like that. They say, "I do it in the flesh, but I don't mean it in my heart. I do it because I am weak in the flesh."

Light and dark cannot exist together. They do not belong together. It is impossible to be in fellowship with God who is light and to live a life that is in the dark at the same time. Amos asks, "Can two walk together, except they be agreed?" (Amos 3:3).

By virtue of the fact that their name is on a church roll, many church members declare, "I am walking with God. I am serving God in the fellowship of the local church and therefore I am on God's side." Yet there are habits in their life that are clearly of the darkness. There are attitudes in their soul that clearly do not belong to the light. Their practice does not measure up to their profession.

C. Prevarication

John says that if we profess one thing and practice another "we lie, and do not the truth" (1 John 1:6). John does not mince words. He would never have won a popularity contest. Never would he have been elected "man of the year." He would never have passed a course on "how to win friends and influence people" (to get me what I want). No, John says that if you say one thing and live another, you are a liar. You are not doing the truth. You are living in prevarication. You are a walking lie. You are acting a lie.

What a terrible thing for a Christian to be living a lie. And sometimes church leaders find themselves in that position. There are leaders in the church who everyone thinks are great. They pretend to be one kind of person on Sunday, yet they are an altogether different person on Monday. They walk with the saints on Sunday and with the sinners on Monday. They talk like the children of God on Sunday and they talk like the children of the world on Monday. They pretend to be one thing and they practice another thing. So they live a lie, a life of prevarication. What a tragedy for anyone to say, "I am a Christian," and yet to live a lie.

When you do that, you do several detrimental things. One, when you live a lie, when you pretend to be in the light but walk in darkness, you misrepresent your Lord. Whatever people say about Jesus Christ, I think they would all agree that Jesus Christ was not a phony. I don't like a phony, do you? I don't like for people to pretend to be something they are not. Jesus Christ was not a phony. His walk matched his talk. He was the real thing. For a Christian, a person who bears the name of Jesus, to walk in darkness is to misrepresent the Lord.

Second, living a lie misdirects the lost. There was a light-house on the Florida coast. When one of the glasses of the lan-

tern was broken, they replaced the glass with tin. In that part of
the lighthouse there was a dark spot. A ship came in one night
in a storm, seeking harbor. The captain looked for the light-
house, saw nothing, and crashed on shore because there was a
dark spot. I wonder if there are lost people who are looking for
the light, for direction, for Jesus Christ, who look at us and see a
dark spot.

III. The Blessing of This Fellowship

A. Walking with God

If we walk in the light as he is in the light, we discover two
blessings (1 John 1:7). If we live a life of obedience to Jesus
Christ, without known, unconfessed sin in our life, scripture says we will have the wonderful blessing of communion
with God.

How are we going to have communion, things in common,
with God? Well, if I am going to walk with God, I am going to
have to know what God likes and dislikes. God has given me a
Bible. It says, "Thy word is a lamp unto my feet, and a light unto
my path" (Psalm 119:105). I read the Bible, I find out what God
likes, and I learn to like that. I find out what God dislikes, and I
learn to dislike that. I learn to have communion and fellowship
with God. I talk to God; he talks with me. I share with God; he
shares with me. That is the greatest thing that can happen to
anyone on this earth.

Some of you are businessmen and women. You are faced with
the pressures of business life. You are faced with the pressures
of a tremendous schedule every day, and you will never really
get through it unless you learn the lesson of walking with God
in your daily life.

A group of natives was going through the jungles with an explorer. The explorer was quite impatient, constantly hurrying,
constantly in a rush, constantly moving. He did not have time to
rest. Finally one morning he got ready to push on through the
jungle and the natives just sat there; they would not move an
inch. The explorer went up to the head of the natives and said,
"What's wrong? Why won't these men move on?" The leader

said, "Sir, you have gone so very fast that our men are going to stop for a while today and let their soul catch up with their body."

We, too, need to do that. Sometimes we need to be still and know that God is God. So, take a few moments at the beginning of the day, before all of the hurry and hectic schedule. Open God's word and have fellowship with God.

B. Washed in the Blood

This passage points to a second blessing, the daily blessing of being washed in the blood of Jesus Christ. Look at the last part of 1 John 1:7. "And the blood of Jesus Christ his Son cleanseth us from all sin." John is not talking about the blood of Jesus Christ in his veins. There was no salvation in the blood of Jesus Christ when that blood remained in his veins. There is no salvation, no heaven, for any person in the perfect life of Jesus Christ. When I see the perfect life Jesus lived, it only condemns me. It only shows me my sin. It only shows me the hopelessness of trying to get to heaven by emulating the example of Jesus Christ.

The blood of Jesus poured out on the cross of Calvary, the blood that was shed, makes it possible for poor hell-deserving lost sinners to go to heaven.

Some people make fun of the blood of Jesus. They say, Don't give me a slaughterhouse religion; don't talk to me about blood. Yet scripture declares, "Without shedding of blood is no remission [of sin]" (Hebrews 9:22). Thank God for the precious blood of Jesus! The Bible says, "Forasmuch as ye know that ye were not redeemed with corruptible things, as silver and gold, from your vain conversation received by tradition from your fathers; But with the precious blood of Christ, as of a lamb without blemish and without spot" (1 Peter 1:18–19).

Scripture says, "Feed the church of God, which he hath purchased with his own blood" (Acts 20:28). When Jesus applied the blood to Calvary's cross, he purchased us from the slave market of sin, redeemed us from the depths of sin, and made it possible for us to go to heaven.

Praise God, the blood is peace-giving blood! Colossians 1:20 says, "Having made peace through the blood of his cross, by him to reconcile all things unto himself; by him, I say, whether they be things in earth, or things in heaven."

The blood is also purging blood. Hebrews 9:14 says, "How much more shall the blood of Christ, who through the eternal Spirit offered himself without spot to God, purge your conscience from dead works to serve the living God?"

Thank God for the prevailing blood! In Revelation 12:11 the Bible says, "They overcame him by the blood of the Lamb." I believe in the blood. Without it there is no salvation. Without it there is no remission.

We must note, too, that John did not just say the blood cleansed (past tense), but the blood cleanseth (present tense). Present tense means that the blood goes on cleansing. An initial cleansing of our sins took place at the cross. Revelation 1:5 says, "Unto him that loved us, and washed us from our sins in his own blood. . . ." In one great redemptive act at the cross of Calvary, Jesus Christ washed us for time and eternity. He washed us forever and it need not be repeated.

However, this passage in 1 John speaks of a continual washing. The blood of Jesus Christ offered on the altar in glory has eternal efficacy. It will never lose its power; it will always cleanse from sin.

Often when you become a Christian and get close to the light, you see the dark spots in your life as you have never seen them before. Somehow when you step out of the darkness into the light you see yourself as you are. Perhaps for the first time you begin to see the depths of your sin. You begin to see how foul and shameful your sins actually are. When Satan brings those sins up before you, isn't it glorious to know that the blood avails, that the blood cleanses even from *that* sin?

Charles Finney was preaching in a great revival in Detroit. After the service one night a man said, "I want you to come home with me, Mr. Finney." Some who knew the man said to Finney, "Don't go," but he went. When they got to the man's house, they walked in, the man locked the door, and pulled a revolver from his pocket. He said, "Don't be afraid, Mr. Finney. I am not going to shoot you. I heard you preach tonight about the Lord Jesus Christ. This revolver has killed four men. Is there any hope for a man like that?"

Mr. Finney replied, "The blood of Jesus Christ his Son cleanses us from all sin."

The man answered, "You don't understand, Mr. Finney.

Down below this apartment where you are sitting there is a saloon. I have helped send men down the road to hell; I have helped men to rob their own children of food and milk. Is there any hope for a man who would run a saloon?"

Mr. Finney replied, "The blood of Jesus Christ his Son cleanses us from all sin."

The man continued, "I have been a gambler all my life. I have spent my life taking money from people illegally. Is there any hope for a man like that?"

Mr. Finney said, "The blood of Jesus Christ his Son cleanses us from all sin."

The man persisted. "Across the street there is a wife I have abused, a little girl who is disfigured. One night I came home from gambling and drinking in a drunken stupor. The child ran to put her arms around me and I pushed her away from me. She hit the heater, and is terribly disfigured. Is there any hope for a man like that?"

Mr. Finney said, "The blood of Jesus Christ his Son cleanses us from all sin."

Soon thereafter Mr. Finney left. The next morning the man stumbled across the street. He had not slept; he had prayed all night. When he got into the house he stumbled up to his room. In a little while his wife said to the little girl, "Tell your daddy it's time for breakfast."

She went upstairs and said, "Mama says it's time for breakfast."

The man said, "Maggie, darling, I don't want any breakfast this morning."

She ran back downstairs and said, "Mama, Daddy said he did not want any breakfast this morning and he called me darling."

The mother said, "You made a mistake; you heard him wrong. Go back up there and tell him it's time for breakfast."

In a moment the man came down, took his wife in his arms and his little girl on his knee. "O wife," he wept, "I have sinned against you like few men have ever sinned against anyone, but last night I heard the preacher preach. I heard about Jesus and about the blood of Jesus. The blood of Jesus has cleansed me from all my sin. You have a new husband. Daughter, you have a new daddy."

Have you been washed in the blood? Has the blood been applied to your heart? Jesus wants to cleanse us from all our sin.

3

What to Do with Our Sins
1 John 1:8–2:2

I. WE CAN COVER OUR SINS
   A. Concealment
   B. Chastisement
II. WE CAN CONFESS OUR SINS
   A. Confession
   B. Cleansing

SIN HINDERS OUR FELLOWSHIP WITH GOD. IF WE SIN, THERE IS NO BREAKING of our sonship relationship to God, but a cloud comes between us; our fellowship with God is broken. It is therefore God's desire that every one of us as Christians should not sin.

John says, "My little children, these things write I unto you, that ye sin not" (1 John 2:1). God does not want us to sin. There is no encouragement whatsoever in the Bible for Christians to sin.

Some people excuse sin and make it less than a serious matter. However, according to the word of God it is a very serious thing when a Christian sins. Because it is not the desire of God for us to sin, he has made provision for daily victory over the practice of sin in our life.

The standard of God could be nothing less than perfection. Jesus said, "Be ye therefore perfect, even as your Father which is in heaven is perfect" (Matthew 5:48). John says first of all, "My little children, I write these things that you sin not." Then he continues, "And if any man sin, we have an advocate with the Father." John is saying that God does not want us to sin, and we need not sin. Provision has been made for us to have victory over sin. Yet it is possible for Christians to disobey the Lord.

James 3:2 says, "In many things we offend all." All of us along the way do things we ought not to do. Would anyone be so presumptuous as to say he or she has never sinned since becoming a Christian? Since we gave our life to Jesus we all have sinned many times; we have broken our heart and the heart of the Lord.

As we study the lives of God's people throughout the word of God, we find that they sometimes sinned. Consider the story of David, a great man, "a man after God's own heart." Yet David committed sin, and brought tragedy and heartache to his life. Consider Moses, a great leader, a man of God in many ways, yet because of the sin of disobedience he was not allowed to go into the promised land. Simon Peter, a man who preached on the day of Pentecost, an intimate disciple of the Lord Jesus Christ, even he denied that he knew the Lord.

At this point the average Christian and especially the young Christian sometimes gets confused about the Christian life. Here is a young Christian who has just received Jesus as personal Savior and very soon after does something he ought not to do. At that moment Satan rushes in to accuse his heart. His conscience also condemns him. He is frustrated and confused. He thinks, "Well, now that I have become a Christian I should not sin anymore." Because sin has entered into his life he grows discouraged and thereafter lives a defeated life as a Christian.

Many people who have had an experience of grace with the Lord Jesus, who really know Christ as their personal Savior, because of sin have the idea that it is hopeless and think that they cannot live for the Lord again and be fruitful in his service.

All of us must be clear about what can be done when we sin. It is entirely possible for us to come to grips with the problem of sin in our life as a Christian, to have victory over it, to recover and be a useful, helpful Christian. We do not have to stay down in the mud. We do not have to remain in the ditch when we disobey God and bring shame on the Savior. It is possible for us to pick up and move on again.

We have two alternatives when sin comes into our life.

I. We Can Cover Our Sins

First of all, when we sin as a Christian we can cover our sin. If
we choose, we can pretend it is not there.

A. Concealment

Verses 6, 8, and 10 of 1 John 1 begin in the same way: "If we
say. . . ." John is showing that it is possible for Christians to cover
their sin by lying. In other words, they say one thing, but they
are really lying because what they are saying is not true.

How does a Christian go about lying when he has sinned? He
lies in three directions. First, when a Christian sins, if he tries to
cover it, he begins by lying to others. Look at 1 John 1:6. "If we
say that we have fellowship with him, and walk in darkness, we
lie, and do not the truth." Here is a person who has let sin come
into his life and he is lying to other people. This is the man who
pretends to be more than he is. He pretends that he is in fellowship with God. He makes believe that he is truly walking with
God. He seeks to get other people to believe that he is all which
he ought to be and that he is close to God. This is what I call
"games Christians play," games of pretending to be what you really are not. You may go to church, you may be active in its organizations and activities, yet you are playing games.

You are pretending to be in fellowship with God when all the
time down in your heart you know you are not actually in fellowship with God. That is a miserable kind of life for a person to
live. You see, he knows he is not right with God and is putting on
a show in front of other people, so he constantly has to be cau-
tious lest he let his real self come out in front of the people he is
trying to deceive.

He begins to live two lives, a church life and another life. He
has a life outside the church. I am talking about a person who
comes to church and sings in the choir. Or he sits in the congregation and folks look at him and say, "My, that man is a fine
Christian," but when he goes back to his place of business and
into his daily activities he has a different life altogether. He has
another vocabulary and different habits. He is living a lie.

I am talking about a young person who is known as one of the
"in" crowd at church. He is known as one of the dedicated, con-

secrated Christians at church, yet when he gets to school he tells the same dirty jokes the rest of the kids tell. He does the same things the lost do. He lives a life of pretense and sham. His life is veneer; he is a phony; he is not the real thing. He is concealing his sin by lying to other people.

But it does not stop there. When you begin to lie to other people about your spiritual condition, you begin to lie to yourself. Look at 1 John 1:8. "If we say that we have no sin, we deceive ourselves, and the truth is not in us." We start off by lying to others, but if we continue to lie we eventually lie to ourselves as well. You must live with yourself. You must live with your own thoughts. If you let sin come into your life as a Christian and you do not confess it and get it out of your life, then you have to play the game of self-deception. You have to pretend that what you are doing is not so bad after all and really there is no sin in your life that needs to be dealt with.

This is why some people are in mental institutions who are really not sick. They are not actually mentally ill but they are trying to deceive themselves. They are not living on the basis of inward reality; they are not being what they really know they are in their own heart. They are lying to themselves.

In this eighth verse, "If we say that we have no sin," the word used for "sin" is a noun. You could translate it, "If we say that we have no sin nature, we deceive ourselves." Do you see what kind of person John is referring to? John is describing the one who denies that he is a sinner by nature. Such a person excuses himself and says, "I am not such a bad guy; I am basically a pretty good fellow."

These are the people who say, "It is not really me that is doing it. It is just my flesh. It is not actually me, but it is that old flesh of mine which gets me into trouble." It is the attitude of the person who says, "The devil made me do it [and therefore the devil is to blame, not me]."

The Bible says that we do have a sin nature. Something is basically wrong at the inner core of our being. David said, "Behold, I was shapen in iniquity; and in sin did my mother conceive me" (Psalm 51:5). We all have something about us that makes us sinners. You are not a sinner because you do sinful things; you do sinful things because you are a sinner. There is within us a root of sin and from that root of sin we produce the fruits of sin.

Take, for example, a dog. You see a dog walking around and in a little while it starts barking. You say, "That dog is a dog because it barks," No, that dog barks because it is a dog. Do you look out at a tree and see the tree has branches and then say, "Well, that tree has branches and therefore it is a tree." No, because it is a tree it has branches. The reason we do things we ought not to do is because we have a sin nature.

When you get to the point that you want to cover sin, you try to excuse yourself and begin to lie to yourself. But that is not where it stops. 1 John 1:10 says, "If we say that we have not sinned, we make him a liar." Do you see the progression of truth here? You start off by lying to others; you live a life of shame before others. Then you begin to lie to yourself; you deceive yourself. If you continue with sin in your life, eventually you will lie to God and deny that you sin at all.

Occasionally I run into people who claim they are sinless. When I was young, I went into a home and tried to talk to a woman about the Lord and his work. She looked at me and said, "Young man, I want you to know I have not sinned in twenty years." There are some folks like that. She was really lying to God.

People call sin by other names. They don't call it lying; it is a "credibility gap." It is not deceit; it is called getting along in your business relationships. It is not adultery, but a harmless escapade. Not anger, but righteous indignation. You no longer call sin what the Bible calls it, and therefore you put yourself in the position of making God a liar. If you do that, you are entitled to know what the Bible says will be the response of God.

B. Chastisement

If you cover your sin, God's response to your life will be chastisement. I do not know where the idea came from, but somewhere along the way people got the idea that if they are Christians they can somehow sin and God is going to overlook it and not punish them simply because they are his child.

In fact, it is more serious when a Christian sins than when a non-Christian sins. When we sin we are bringing shame on the

name of the Lord Jesus, and God will not let us get away with it.
God loves us too much to permit us to sin and get away with it.

I call Hebrews 12 "the Bible woodshed." I don't know how
many modern boys and girls know what the woodshed is, but
the old-timers do. This passage has to do with how God deals
with his children when they sin. Hebrews 12:5–6 says, "And ye
have forgotten the exhortation which speaketh unto you as
unto children." The writer then quotes from the book of Proverbs. "My son, despise not thou the chastening of the Lord, nor
faint when thou art rebuked of him: For whom the Lord loveth
he chasteneth, and scourgeth every son whom he receiveth."
When we are chastised as Christians, it is proof that God really
loves us.

My father believed there were only two ways to handle a
child. If he did good, pat him on the back and if he did bad, pat
him on the back—a little lower. He used to say to me, "Son, this
is hurting me a lot more than it is you." I know now what he was
talking about. If a father truly loves his son, he is not going to be
content to stand by and watch things enter his life that will keep
him from being all that he could be. God loves us and when we
sin he will deal with our sin.

Hebrews 12:7 says, "If ye endure chastening, God dealeth
with you as with sons; for what son is he whom the father
chasteneth not?" Every time I bring a message like this, about
sin in the life of a believer and God's chastening us when we sin,
I get the feeling that some people sitting in the congregation try
to turn the whole thing off. They look off in space somewhere
and think about something else. They try not to listen because
they don't believe what I am saying. They are really saying
down inside themselves, "That preacher is crazy; I am sinning
and I am getting by. I am doing wrong things, and I am not being
chastened. I am making a good salary; I am living high; everything is going well with me. It is not bothering me to sin." But if
you study this passage carefully you discover that God chastens
only those who are his children. The next verse goes on to say
that if you do not experience chastening, if you are sinning and
getting by, then you are not a son. It is evidence that you are really not in the family of God, for God chastens only those who
are members of his family.

"Furthermore we have had fathers of our flesh which corrected us, and we gave them reverence: shall we not much rather be in subjection unto the Father of spirits, and live? For they verily for a few days chastened us after their own pleasure; but he for our profit, that we might be partakers of his holiness. Now no chastening for the present seemeth to be joyous, but grievous" (Hebrews 12:9–11). The writer is saying that while chastening is going on, it hurts. "Nevertheless afterward it yieldeth the peaceable fruit of righteousness unto them which are exercised thereby." When it is over, we have been brought back to the Lord, sin has been dealt with in our life, and we have been made a better and a more mature Christian because of the experience.

The chastisement of God can take many forms. Sometimes God chastens people physically because of their sin. I do not believe that all sickness is because of sin nor do I believe that every time someone gets sick it is because they have not had enough faith in God or because they are out of the will of God. I do not believe that every person in the hospital is there because God is chastening them, but I do believe that many people experience physical difficulties because they are out of the will of God. God is chastening them and trying to bring them back to him. David nearly died when sin was in his life. In Psalm 32:4 David talked about that experience and said, "Day and night thy hand was heavy upon me." It nearly killed him. Sometimes the chastening will be physical.

Sometimes the chastening will come in forms of mental oppression. God may disturb you mentally because of your sin. Think about Lot. Lot was down in Sodom, compromised and worldly in his daily life. Do you know what Peter says about Lot? "For that righteous man dwelling among them, in seeing and hearing, vexed his righteous soul from day to day with their unlawful deeds" (2 Peter 2:8). What was wrong? God was disturbing Lot mentally.

One of the results when we let sin harbor in our heart is that it affects us spiritually. Think about Simon Peter when the sin of denying the Lord Jesus Christ came into his life. He lost the joy of salvation. He was warming himself at the devil's fire and when he saw the look of his Savior it broke his heart. Why? The chastening of God touched him spiritually and he saw his sin.

How does God go about chastening us? Revelation 3:19 says,

"As many as I love, I rebuke and chasten." Do you see the order there? God says first, "I will rebuke," and second, "I will chasten."

Suppose one day my boys are out in the front yard. As boys are known to do, they get into a little fuss. I go outside and say, "All right, boys, no fussing out here. I want you to be sweet and good boys." I have rebuked them a little. I go back in the house and everything is all right for about five minutes. Then there they are, out there fussing again. I go out again. "Now listen, boys. I have already warned you one time. I am not going to have this fussing out here. It is not right, and you had better stop or Daddy is going to have to do something else." I go back in the house and things are all right for about ten minutes. The next thing I hear is snarling and fighting like cats and dogs. So Daddy goes out again and says, "All right, boys, I came out here twice and I rebuked you. The rebuke did not seem to do the job so I am going to have to take you into the house and solve the problem inside."

Turn to 1 Corinthians 11:30, a verse that ought to scare you to death if you are a Christian with sin in your life. Paul is talking about Christians who have sin in their life and are misbehaving in the house of God. "For this cause [that is, because of sin in their life] many are weak and sickly among you, and many sleep." That does not mean physical sleep. It means because of sin many have died. Some Christians shorten their stay on this earth because they let sin get in their life and they cover it and refuse to let God get it out of their life. Because they are truly born-again believers and because that sin in their life hinders their testimony and effectiveness for the Lord, and they refuse his rebuke, God says, "All right, I will have to take you up to my big house in heaven and remove your inconsistent testimony from this earth." It is a serious thing when we let unconfessed sin stay in our life. We are on dangerous ground.

II. We Can Confess Our Sins

A. Confession

Your first alternative is that you can cover your sin by lying to others, by lying to yourself, and by lying to God. If you do, God says, "I will chastise you." But you have another alternative! It is also possible for Christians to confess our sins.

"He that covereth his sins shall not prosper" (Proverbs 28:13). If there is sin in your life as a Christian you will not prosper. Nothing you do will come out right. Almost every move you make will cause a problem. "But whoso confesseth and forsaketh them shall have mercy."

God's alternative is to confess our sins. "If we confess our sins, he is faithful and just to forgive us our sin and to cleanse us from all unrighteousness" (1 John 1:9).

Some people want to use 1 John 1:9 as a kind of spiritual rabbit's foot to give them something to turn to when they sin. They may say to themselves, "I can go ahead and do this because God will forgive me. God will let me by."

What does it mean to confess? It is more than just saying, "I am sorry." The Greek word for "confess" means "to say the same thing." When you confess sin it means you are saying the same thing about sin that God says about it. It means you are agreeing with God about sin.

This is why people do not confess sin. They do not agree with God about it. They do not call it what God calls it. People pray, "*If* I have sinned." Come on now! What do you mean, "If I have sinned"? Why pray if you are not sure about it? Why pray until you know you have sinned?

You don't know what you have done? You don't know what your sins are? That is why you don't get it right; you do not agree with God about it. You do not call it what God calls it; you do not say the same thing about it. That is why people do not give up sin.

I am tired of hearing people disagree with what God calls sin. They want to call it love. They come to my study and spill out the same old story about having an affair with somebody.

Now there is not a way in the world that such a relationship can be love. What people call love is what God calls lust. They will never get peace in their heart until they are willing to call it what God calls it. When they begin to see it in the light in which God has revealed it in the Bible and begin to see it for the terrible thing it is in their life, they will have a holy abhorrence for it.

The Bible says, "Whoso confesseth and forsaketh it. . . ." That word *forsake* means to let go, to turn it loose. You will never turn it loose until you see it for what it is. That is why some folks don't quit using tobacco. They have never called it what God calls it, "defiling the temple of the Holy Spirit." That is why some of you cannot get rid of your pride. You never call it what God calls it. You may think you are so much deeper in the things of God than others, and God says it is pride. Quit whitewashing it. Quit perfuming it. Call it what God calls it.

A little child got his hand caught in a vase, and the parents did everything they could to try to get that child's hand out. As a last resort, they broke the vase and when they did they discovered the child had a nickel doubled up in his fist. The reason God cannot get sin out of your life is because you are holding onto it and you secretly love it. But, praise God, you can confess it. You can quit playing mental games, you can quit putting on airs in front of people, you can quit lying to God, you can quit excusing your sins. You can confess them.

B. Cleansing

When you confess your sin as a born-again child of God, a number of things begin to take place in the unseen spirit world. Every time we sin we have an accuser; we have a prosecuting attorney who demands the death penalty because of our sin. Revelation 12:10 says, "And I heard a loud voice saying in heaven, Now is come salvation, and strength, and the kingdom of our God, and the power of his Christ: for the accuser of our brethren is cast down, which accused them before our God day and night." When we sin, that old dragon, that old devil, goes rushing into the presence of God and begins to accuse us. "There he is, there is your Christian. Look at him. On the basis of the wages of sin, I demand the death penalty."

But 1 John 2:1 says we also have an advocate. "If any man sin, we have an advocate." The Greek word for *advocate* means one who is called alongside to plead our case.

In fact, we really have two advocates. We have two lawyers to take up our case. We each have an advocate in our heart. When Jesus promised the coming of the Holy Spirit he said he would be the comforter. It is the same Greek word. In other words, we have an advocate in our heart who is the personal representative of God the Father. When we sin, God's advocate in our heart pleads his case in our heart. When we sin, God's advocate in our heart begins to convict us of our sin, and we get miserable.

We also have an advocate in heaven. The Lord Jesus, the righteous and faithful one, is the advocate at the right hand of the throne of God.

So, the accuser of the brethren, the devil, rushes in. He demands the death penalty and says, "Look at him; look at her." Then the Lord Jesus says, "Yes, Father, but look at me. On the basis of my shed blood, I plead for the remission of that sin." Thank God, the blood avails. "He is faithful and just to forgive us our sin." He cleanses us.

Now consider 1 John 2:2: "And he is the propitiation." The word *propitiation* in the Old Testament is "mercy seat." The mercy seat was that golden slab over the broken law of God where the blood was applied. We have an advocate on the basis of the blood poured out on the cross of Calvary. Because he is the propitiation for our sins, we can be forgiven when we sin and God will send our sins away from us.

Remember when you were little and told your mother a fib? Remember how bad you felt, how miserable you were? You could not stand to be away from Mama, yet you could not stand to be with her. Finally, you just couldn't stand it anymore, and you ran to her and confessed it all and said, "Mama, I am so sorry. I want you to forgive me. Please, I am so sorry." Do you remember how she took you into her arms and smothered you with kisses? You were back in fellowship. That is the way it is when a Christian sins, and confesses it, and is brought back into fellowship with God.

If you are a lost person, however, not a word of this applies to your sin. If you are lost, every time you sin you are piling up wrath against the judgment day of God. You have no advocate; you have no propitiation. But Jesus said that he died for the sins of the whole world and he is the propitiation for the whole world. He died for you and if you will come to Jesus, if you will come with that load of your sin, he will wash you as white as snow.

4

Old, Yet New
1 John 2:3–11

I. ATTITUDE
   A. Obedience Desired
   B. Obedience Described
   C. Obedience Discharged
II. ACTIONS
   A. The Walk of the Savior
   B. The Walk of the Saint
III. AFFECTION
   A. Essence
   B. Example
   C. Experience

AMONG THE MANY PURPOSES OF THE BOOK OF 1 JOHN, THE MAIN ONE IS that you and I might come to know that we are truly children of God, know that we are born again. The Bible teaches that Christians can know they are saved. In 2 Timothy 1:12 the Bible says, "For I know whom I have believed, and am persuaded that he is able to keep that which I have committed unto him against that day." In 1 John 5:13 scripture says, "These things have I written unto you that believe on the name of the Son of God; that ye may know that ye have eternal life." I cannot imagine going to one of the first-century Christians, asking if he or she were saved, and receiving the reply, "Well, I think I am saved or I hope I am saved or maybe I am saved." Those early Christians had assurance because their salvation was based on a real experience with the Lord Jesus Christ and the unshakable testimony of the word of God.

First John is given specifically to make it possible for Christians to know that they are saved. "And hereby we do know that we know him, if we keep his commandments" (1 John 2:3). In these five chapters the word *know* is used some thirty-nine times. It refers to experiential knowledge.

In verse 4, John begins, "He that saith, I know him, and keepeth not his commandments. . . ." In verse 6 we see the same phrase again: "He that saith he abideth in him ought himself also so to walk, even as he walked." Again in verse 9 that little phrase occurs: "He that saith he is in the light, and hateth his brother, is in darkness even until now." John uses that phrase "he that saith" three times. He is using it to introduce us to a series of tests by which we can know beyond a doubt that we are a child of God.

It is one thing to say that something is true; it is an altogether different thing for it actually to be true. It would be possible for me to say, "I am a bird, I am a bird, I am a bird," but that would not make it so. Saying that you are a child of God does not make it so. A person may say, "Lord, Lord," yet scripture says that Jesus can reply, "I never knew you" (Matthew 7:23). It is not enough just to say that you are saved.

I. Attitude

The first test to help you know whether you are truly a child of God is in 1 John 2:3–5, the test of attitude.

A. Obedience Desired

John begins by saying, "And hereby we do know that we know him, if we keep his commandments" (1 John 2:3). The word *keep* is an interesting word that means to guard carefully, as if a person were guarding a treasure. A person who is genuinely born again will have an attitude that desires to guard and keep the commandments of God. It is not enough for someone just to claim to be saved. There must be an attitude of obedience in his or her heart.

John is blunt and specific. "He that saith, I know him, and keepeth not his commandments, is a liar, and the truth is not in him" (1 John 2:4). I would not risk calling you a liar, yet John says that if you say you know the Lord but there is not an attitude of obedience in your heart, you are a liar and God's truth is not in you. John does not mean we will live a life of perfect obedience to the commandments of God. Not one of us would say we have always perfectly kept the commandments of God. But he does mean that we will have an attitude of really wanting to do what God wants us to do. The lost man or woman has no desire for the things of God. Unregenerate souls have no interest in finding out what God wants them to be and to do. But the new- birth experience puts into our heart a desire really and actually to do what God wants.

B. Obedience Described

First John 2:3 says, "Hereby we do know that we know him, if we keep his commandments." Underline the word *commandments*. Verse 5 starts out, "But whoso keepeth his word. . . ." Underline *word*. Do you see the difference? In one verse John talks about keeping the commandments of God; in the other verse he talks about keeping the word of God. There is a difference.

In John 14:15 our Savior says, "If ye love me, keep my commandments." There it is again. One of the evidences that we love the Lord is that we will want to keep the commandments of God. In John 14:23 the Lord says, "If a man love me, he will keep my words." He says, first of all, keep my commandments and, second, keep my word. Again we come upon a difference between wanting to do the commandments of God and wanting to do the word of God.

As an illustration, suppose a teenager comes home from school and his mother says something like this, "Bill, I want you to be sure to take out the garbage for me and I want you to wash the car." Those are specific commandments of his mother. If Bill wants to obey his mother, he will obey the commandments specifically given him. That is a matter of commandments. But suppose the next day Bill comes home and overhears his mother talking to a friend. His mother says, "Well, I am not feeling so well today and I do wish I had someone to clean up the house for me. I wish I had someone to wash the dishes for me." Bill cleans up the house and washes the dishes for his mother—not because he is commanded to do so, but because he loves her and wants to do not only her commandments, but also her word. This is the attitude that will be in the heart of the child of God.

We open up the word of God and find certain specific commandments of God. If we are saved, we will desire to obey those commandments of God. But also, as we read the Bible, we run across some of the desires of Jesus. They are not specific commandments, but as we read we learn that this is what pleases Jesus; this is what Jesus really wants us to be. Because we have come to know him, because we love him, we keep not only his commandments, but also his words.

C. Obedience Discharged

John says, "But whoso keepeth his word, in him verily is the love of God perfected" (1 John 2:5). If we really love God and if God's love accomplishes its intention, reaches its goal, in our heart, we will have an attitude of obedience to the commandments and to the word of God.

So, the first test of salvation is the test of attitude. What is your attitude toward the word of God? How do you look at the commandments of God and the desires of God? If there is constant rebellion in your heart, if there is no desire whatsoever in your heart really to do the will of God, then there is a question about your salvation experience. But if deep in your heart you can say, "Lord, I know I am not perfect and I know I fail you sometimes, yet down in my heart I really want to do your will," that is an evidence that you are a child of God. That is the first test, the test of attitude.

II. ACTIONS

The second test is in 1 John 2:6, the test of actions. "He that saith he abideth in him ought himself also so to walk, even as he walked." If you are a child of God, there is a sense of obligation

on your part to live as Jesus lived. Our walk and our talk ought
to coincide; what we say with our lips ought to be consistent
with the way we live our life.

I read about an evangelist who preached back in the days
when they had enough religion to get happy in the services and
shout. This evangelist appointed a shouting committee for his
meetings. Every time anyone shouted in the meeting the committee would investigate the life of those persons the next
week. If the way they lived was consistent with the Christian
life, if their life was really what it ought to be, then they were
permitted to continue shouting. But if it was not, they would
not let them shout in the meeting anymore. Do you see the
point? Our talk ought to match our walk.

A. The Walk of the Savior

We are told that we ought to walk as Jesus walked. Martin
Luther said it is not the walk of the Savior in walking on the
water that is intended here; none of us can walk on the water.
But it is one's everyday, down-to-earth ordinary walk in the
common experiences of life.

Think about the walk of Jesus. Think about the walk of his
childhood, when he walked as a boy in submission to his parents. Think about the walk of his manhood, when he walked up
and down the dusty roads of Galilee and went everywhere
doing good. Think about his walk of saviorhood, when he stead-
fastly set his face to go to Jerusalem.

B. The Walk of the Saint

To walk as he walked means that we ought to desire to imitate
the life of the Lord Jesus—not that salvation is a matter of imi-
tating the Lord Jesus Christ. We are not saved because we try to
emulate him.

Salvation is not imitation; it is identification. We must be
identified with him in his death, in his burial, and in his resurrection, not only for salvation but also for victory in the daily
Christian life. The truth of identification is clearly delineated
in the word of God. But it is also taught in the Bible that we are

to imitate the Son of God once we have been identified with him by faith.

"For even hereunto were ye called: because Christ also suffered for us, leaving us an example, that ye should follow his steps" (1 Peter 2:21). That is imitation. We are to seek to follow the steps of the Lord Jesus Christ everyday. Ephesians 5:1 says, "Be ye therefore followers of God, as dear children." The Greek word translated "followers" is related to our English word *mimic* or *imitator*. Be imitators, be mimics of God, as dear children.

Have you ever seen a little boy trying to imitate his father? Have you ever seen that little fellow trying to walk in the big steps of his daddy? That ought to cause many a man to examine where his steps are leading those little fellows who are following him.

Have you ever seen a little girl try to mimic her mother? Have you ever seen her get on Mama's dress and Mama's high-heeled shoes and go wobbling down the street? What is she doing? She is trying to mimic her parent. She wants to be just like her. That is the way we ought to be if we know him, if we love him.

One of the greatest novels ever written is *In His Steps*. The whole thrust of the book is simply this. A group of people in a church began to try to do what they thought Jesus would do in every situation. It changed their life. It revolutionized their total approach to life. You and I as Christians ought to walk as Jesus walked.

III. Affection

The third test is the test of affection. Your love will be an indication of whether or not you are really a born-again child of God. "Brethren, I write no new commandment unto you." In verse 3 John used the word *commandments*, plural, talking about the commandments of God in general. Now he has narrowed down our thinking to one commandment. That is what the Bible does.

On one occasion a man came to Jesus and asked, "Master, what is the greatest commandment of all?" Jesus distilled all of God's commandments into two. The first commandment, he said, is to love God with all your heart, soul, strength, mind, and

body. The second commandment is "Thou shalt love thy neighbor." Then the apostle Paul in Romans 13:10 distilled those two
commandments into one and said, "Love is the fulfilling of the
law." When John talks about the new commandment he is talking about the commandment of love.

A. Essence

"Brethren, I write no new commandment unto you, but an
old commandment which ye had from the beginning. The old
commandment is the word which ye have heard from the beginning" (1 John 2:7). Now look at verse 8 for a shocker. "Again, a
new commandment I write unto you." That seems to be a contradiction, does it not? He says, I am not going to give you a new
one, it is an old one. And then he turns right around and says, I
am going to give you a new one. What does he mean?

This is one of the wonderful paradoxes in the word of God,
one of those things that seem to be contradictory, yet are not.
There is a sense in which the commandment of love is very old.
One of the basic definitions of God is found in 1 John 4:8: "God is
love." Since the beginning of time, human beings have known
that they were to love, and when Jesus came into this world he
again enunciated the commandment of love.

In John 13:34-35 Jesus says, "A new commandment I give
unto you, That ye love one another; . . . By this shall all men
know that ye are my disciples, if ye have love one to another."
There is a sense in which this love of God is new; the love of God
is new to a soul who experiences it for the first time.

Take the sun. How old is the sun? Why, it is almost as old as
creation itself. Yet when you and I walk out underneath the
warm rays of that sun, we feel a warmth that makes it new to us
all over again. The love of God is like that. The saints of God
have been enjoying his love through the ages. All of God's people through the centuries have rejoiced in his love. But if you
have never experienced the love of God in your own heart, the
first time that love comes flooding into your soul, it is something brand new to you. It is old and yet it is new.

It is interesting to watch young people around church. They
get to certain stages and one of those stages is the puppy-love
stage. I think the puppy-love stage has moved down a little. It

did not hit people of my age until we were fifteen or sixteen. Now it hits at eleven or twelve or thirteen. She looks over at that boy and it just does something to him. His heart starts doing flip flops and he feels as if he's on an elevator. You would think they had just invented love. But love has been around a long, long time. That is the way it is with this new commandment of love, this new experience of the love of God.

If you have never experienced God's love in your heart, you do not know what love is. You have no capacity for love until Jesus comes into your heart and into your life. Love is new to the soul that experiences it for the first time, but it is also new in its emphasis.

There is a new emphasis on love in the New Testament. In the Old Testament the word of God was on the basis of law; God spoke to his children through law. He commanded them to do certain things. In the New Testament there is a different emphasis. The emphasis now is not on the commandment but on the love that fulfills the commandment. That is a greater way to live. It is a lot better to live under love than to live under law. If you live by love, then you are not disturbed by law.

There is a law that says a mother and father have to take care of their children. In the morning, does a Christian man nudge his wife and say, "Get up and feed the children. If you don't, the cops will be down here and arrest us in a little while"? Is that the way you operate? Why, of course not. Why do you feed your children? Why do you clothe your children? Why do you take care of your children? Is it because the law demands that you do so? Of course not. It is because you are living by a higher law, the law of love. It is a new commandment in the sense that it is new in its emphasis.

B. Example

"Again, a new commandment I write unto you, which thing is true in him and in you" (1 John 2:8). This love is true in him. When Jesus came into the world and started loving as only he could, it was something new on the face of this earth. This world had never seen such a display of the love of God as Jesus gave in his everyday life. Oh, how Jesus loved people. I think about how Jesus loved his twelve disciples. How ugly they could be. They would argue with one another, they were filled with self-seeking, selfishness, and littleness of disposition; yet when you read the four gospels you see that Jesus Christ just kept on loving them. He loved them to the point that one day the love of God was real in their heart.

He loved other people too. No one ever felt uncomfortable around Jesus. No one ever felt ill at ease or embarrassed around Jesus. The poorest of the poor, the lowest of sinners—all could feel the warmth of the love of Jesus Christ.

Jesus laid down his life not only for his friends, he laid down his life for his foes. The greatest accusation they could bring against him was this: he is a friend of sinners. This world had never seen such an example of love.

C. Experience

"He that saith he is in the light, and hateth his brother, is in darkness even until now. He that loveth his brother abideth in the light, and there is none occasion of stumbling in him" (1 John 2:9–10). Do you see the contrast between light and darkness, between love and hatred? Those things do not mix. They are mutually exclusive. It is impossible for light and darkness to exist in the same place. It is impossible for love and hate to exist in the same heart. The person who says, "I am in the light, I am saved," yet has hatred in his heart, is in darkness. You cannot hate anybody. You cannot allow hatred in your heart toward any other human being.

If you claim you are in the light, if you claim you are a child of God, and if you hate anyone because of face, place, or race, the Bible says you are walking in darkness. You cannot have hate and love in your heart at the same time.

If there is a place in all the world where love ought to be demonstrated, it is among the people of God. Where is this world going to find love if it does not find it among Christians? They are not going to find it out in the world. Talk about dog- eat-dog, talk about animosity, this world is filled with it. The only place poor sinful human beings can find love is to find it flowing out of the hearts of God's people who have walked out of darkness into the light of salvation.

I want to point out three things. First, if you have hate in your heart, you live in darkness: "He that hateth his brother is in darkness, and walketh in darkness" (1 John 2:11). If you take a flower and put it in the dark, it will shrivel. Take a soul and let it live in the darkness of hate and that soul will become ugly and drab and dull. If you hate, you live in darkness.

Second, if you hate, you walk in darkness: " . . . and walketh in darkness, and knoweth not whither he goeth." If we are walking in darkness we do not know where we are going. When we have hate in our heart, there is no telling what we will do. Who knows where that hatred will lead us? Jesus said, If you have anger in your heart against your brother without a cause, you have committed murder already in your heart. The first step of murder is hatred in your heart.

Third, you grope in darkness: " . . . because that darkness hath blinded his eyes." In the subterranean streams of caves, there are fish which have lived in darkness so long that they have no eyes. Little pit ponies who hauled the coal out of the mines spent so much time down in the darkness that they were blind. And how tragic is a soul that walks in the darkness of hatred. Is there anybody on this earth that you hate?

There is only one hope for blind eyes. When the blind man came to Jesus, our Lord said, "What wilt thou that I shall do unto thee?" The blind man said to Jesus, "Lord, that I may receive my sight." Are you in the darkness? Is your heart filled with bitterness? There is only one hope for you, and that is to let the love of God come flooding in, removing hate. Let the light of God come pouring in, dispelling darkness.

A man came to the Moody Tabernacle in Chicago many years ago. In front of the Tabernacle in gas flames was the scripture, "God is love." This man came into the building that night with his life filled with hatred, bitterness, and sin. He sat through the service, and when the invitation hymn was given he rushed down the aisle to receive Christ as Savior. After the service Mr. Moody went up to him and said, "Sir, what was it about the sermon that caused you to give your heart to Christ tonight?" He said, "It was not anything about the sermon; I hardly heard a word of it." "What song was it?" Mr. Moody then asked. The man replied, "I hardly heard the singing; I don't know a thing they sang tonight." Mr. Moody continued, "Well, what was it? What did it?" The man pointed up to the front and said, "It was that sign up there—God is love. I could not get away from it. God is love, and it broke my heart. For the first time in my life I have love instead of hatred in my heart."

Do you want love in your heart? Jesus stands knocking at your heart's door and he can come flooding in with love, removing hate from your heart.

5

Growing Up
1 John 2:12–14

    I. SPIRITUAL INFANCY
       A. Normal
       B. Abnormal
   II. SPIRITUAL ADOLESCENCE
       A. Strength
       B. Secret
       C. Success
  III. SPIRITUAL MATURITY
       A. Procreation
       B. Confrontation
       C. Illustration

THE SALVATION EXPERIENCE IS PRESENTED MANY TIMES IN THE BIBLE IN terms of a birth experience. Our Savior said, "Ye must be born again" (John 3:7). In 1 Peter 1:23 the Bible says, "Being born again, not of corruptible seed, but of incorruptible, by the word of God, which liveth and abideth forever." James 1:18 says, "Of his own will begat he us with the word of truth, that we should be a kind of firstfruits of his creatures." When a man realizes that he is lost, needs Jesus, repents of his sin, and puts his personal faith in the Lord Jesus Christ, at that moment he is born again and becomes a member of the family of God.

With this in mind, John says, "I write unto you, little children. . . ." The two English words "little children" are actually one word in Greek, meaning "born ones." It comes from a verb meaning "to birth" or "to bring into existence," and is a general term of endearment to describe all of the people of God. If you are a member of the family of God, you are included in this term of endearment. In the book of 1 John, we find this term over and over again; it is John's customary way of greeting all those who are members of the family of God.

Children of God have at least one thing in common. "I write unto you, little children, because your sins are forgiven you for his name's sake" (1 John 2:12). Some of us are young; others are old. We are at different stages of spiritual development. Yet if we are God's children, all of us have experienced forgiven sin.

It is wonderful to know that our sins are forgiven. We used to sing a little chorus, "Gone, gone, gone, gone. Yes, my sins are gone." It is wonderful to read what the Bible says about our sins. When God forgives our sins, he casts them behind his back (Isaiah 38:17). He sees them no more. God removes our sin "as far as the east is from the west" (Psalm 103:12). If you are a Christian you have the joy of knowing that your sins are forgiven.

Notice also the basis of the forgiveness of sin. Why is it possible to say that our sins are forgiven? They are forgiven "for his name's sake." We are forgiven because of what Jesus has done. When Jesus went to the cross of Calvary he was without sin. Yet on that cross he took all our sin burden and God judged it fully and finally. Because of what Jesus has done we have the forgiveness of sin.

Being born into the family of God brings the privilege of sins forgiven. Birth is only the beginning of life, is it not? If birth is normal, we can expect growth. This is true in the spiritual as well as the physical realm. "But grow in grace, and in the knowledge of our Lord and Savior Jesus Christ" (2 Peter 3:18). God wants us to move from spiritual babyhood all the way to maturity in the Lord Jesus.

Ephesians 4:15 says, " . . . but speaking the truth in love, may grow up into him in all things, which is the head, even Christ." That is God's desire for every one of his children. God wants us to grow up into him. The goal of growth for God's children is that we grow to become like Jesus.

Jesus is the only one who ever lived on this earth who in

every way pleased God the Father. He was everything God wanted him to be. God was so pleased with Jesus that he determined to people eternity with replicas of his Son. When God birthed you into his family, it was his divine intention to conform you one day to the image of his Son. In between that birth experience and final maturity there is intended to be a growth process, an experience of growing in grace and becoming more and more what God wants us to be.

These verses give marvelous insights into the psychology of Christian growth. Here we have recorded for us the three stages of spiritual development for God's children.

I. SPIRITUAL INFANCY

This scripture begins with spiritual fathers, talks about spiritual young men, and then spiritual children. I am going to reverse the process and begin with spiritual infancy. In 1 John 2:13 we again note the phrase, "little children." A different word is used here, a word meaning "those who are infants in the Lord," those who are spiritually immature.

What does John say about those who are babies in Jesus? "I write unto you, little children [spiritual infants], because ye have known the Father." That is about all a baby knows when he or she is born into the world: There are some faces, a Mama and a Daddy, and that is about as far as it goes.

When I came to the Lord Jesus Christ at the age of nine, I did not know much about salvation. I did not even begin to understand what was involved in my salvation experience. If you had said to me, "Explain the doctrine of repentance," I could not have done it. If you had said, "Explain what it means to be born of God's Spirit," I could not have done that. If you had said, "Give me the definition of saving faith," I could not. I had received Jesus as my Savior and I had become a member of God's family. That is all I knew.

"Little children, you have known the Father." That is what salvation is. It is getting to know God. Salvation is being born into the family of God and becoming aware of the presence of God in your life. That is all new Christians know. They do not have a spiritual vocabulary, but they know the heavenly Father.

A. Normal

In the spiritual realm two kinds of babies are mentioned. First of all, the Bible talks about normal babies. There are several characteristics of a baby. First, a baby needs love and security. Second, a baby wants for itself, or a baby is selfish. When a little baby is born into the world, all that baby knows how to do is cry and open its mouth. It wants food for itself and does not care if there is anyone else in the world. It is totally self-centered. Third, a baby has the potential of development and growth under normal circumstances.

Every church ought to know the joy of having spiritual babies in its midst. Nothing will put more life, excitement, and joy in a congregation of people than to have a multitude of new Christians in its congregation. You have not lived until you have lots of children around your house! We have four in our home. Let a couple have their first child and Daddy has a big smile on his face, sends roses to Mama, and tells everybody he knows that he has a new daughter or son.

That is the way it ought to be in a church. That is the way God wants it to be. A church, if it is the kind of church it ought to be, must be vitally concerned with spiritual obstetrics. It must be interested in birthing children into God's family. There is only one way a church is going to experience birthing spiritual babies and it is what Isaiah said, "As soon as Zion travailed, she brought forth her children." Our church services ought to be delivery rooms where children are born into the family of God. Sunday after Sunday, service after service, there ought to be those who are newborn into God's family through the ministry and concern of a local church.

A church must also be interested in spiritual pediatrics. A baby is intended to grow. It is a tragedy for a child to be born into the world and never to grow. It is a terrible thing for a man and woman to bring a child into the world and never nurture and develop and mature that child. What a tragedy it is in the spiritual realm for a church to bring newborn babes into the family of God and never feed them and help them grow and mature in Christian life.

We have a responsibility to new Christians. That is what our church training program is all about. This is what the courses for new members are all about. We are involved in pediatrics, in spiritual development. We are helping babies grow and mature in the Lord.

How do you help babies grow? There are at least four essentials if they are to grow normally.

First, babies must have food. Some of the saddest things I have ever seen are pictures of babies starving to death because of malnutrition. The same thing is true in the spiritual realm. The reason some people stay babies is that they never get spiritual food. As 1 Peter 2:2 says, "As newborn babes, desire the sincere milk of the word, that ye may grow thereby." You must have the word of God. A baby must have spiritual food. We have to feed them the word of God.

If you are a new Christian, the most important habit you can form in your life is to begin daily, diligently, and discerningly to study the word of God. I suggest that you start with the milk of the word and not the strong meat. You do not bring babies home and say, "All right now, kid, get up to the table. We're serving T-bone steaks for supper." That is not the way it is done. You begin with milk and when the baby grows a little bit, you move on to cereal. Then you move on to other food. After teeth are there you are able to give more solid food.

Start with the simplest truths of the Bible, the ABCs, the milk of the word of God. Don't start in the book of Leviticus, Ezekiel, Revelation. Start with the four gospels. Read the story of the Lord Jesus Christ. It will build spiritual strength.

Second, babies must have air. The air of the spiritual baby is prayer, talking to God. Just as we need oxygen in order to live, so do we need communication with our heavenly Father. Talk to God in prayer everyday.

Third, babies must have exercise. This is also true in the spiritual realm. If you are going to grow as a Christian you need to start doing something for God. If you don't have a job, go to a Christian bookstore, get some tracts, and start passing them out. Knock on doors. Do something for Jesus Christ. Get some exercise; it will help you grow.

A fourth essential of spiritual growth is a proper atmosphere. You would not bring a baby home, put him out on the porch, and say, "All right, kid, do the best you can. We are not going to bring you into the warmth of the house. We are going to let you shift for yourself out there and if it gets cold that is just your tough luck." You don't do it that way, do you? You bring a baby into an atmosphere of warmth. And the only place a newborn Christian is going to find the kind of spiritual warmth he or she needs is in a local church of born-again believers where the psychology of spiritual development is understood, where the newborn can be nurtured in their Christian faith, where they can have the understanding, concern, and friendliness that are essential to growth. I have never seen people really mature in their Christian life apart from a vital connection with a local church. If you separate yourself from a local church, you circumvent one of the ways God uses to make you grow.

B. Abnormal

Another kind of baby is mentioned in the word of God, the abnormal one. Nothing is sadder than a baby that does not grow. Babies are cute for a while, but they are not cute if they stay babies. Maternity wings in hospitals are not intended to become rest homes. Wouldn't it be a sight if you went to a maternity ward in one of our hospitals, and there a nurse is sitting in a rocking chair and in her arms is a forty-year-old man with his thumb in his mouth. You ask, "Who is that?" "This is a baby who was born here forty years ago and he liked it so well he decided to stay." That illustration does paint a silly spectacle, but did you know that in 1 Corinthians 3 a similar picture is presented?

In 1 Corinthians Paul was dealing with a group of people who claimed to be spiritual, yet they were the worldliest crowd in the New Testament. They claimed to have all kinds of spiritual gifts. They claimed they were further along spiritually than anyone else. But when Paul wrote to them and dealt with some of the heresies and errors that had crept into their spiritual home, their church, he said, "I, brethren, could not speak unto you as unto spiritual, but as unto carnal, even as unto babes in Christ." Spiritual babies—they had never matured. They were not growing in the Lord. Their growth was stunted. They were abnormal.

Are you still in your spiritual infancy? Have you grown in the Lord?

II. Spiritual Adolescence

In 1 John 2:14 the words "young men" refer to what I call spiritual adolescence. God wants us to begin to grow, to move toward Christian maturity. He says three things about this stage.

A. Strength

First, John says, "I have written unto you, young men, because ye are strong" (1 John 2:14). One of the characteristics of youth is its strength. Young persons can run a marathon; they can hang in there almost indefinitely. They have unbounded energy. The young are strong, and one of the characteristics of spiritual adolescence is strength.

The Bible tells us we need to be strong in many ways. The Son of God "waxed strong in spirit." Are you strong in spirit? The Bible says Abraham was strong in faith, and all of us are urged in Ephesians 6:10 to "be strong in the Lord, and in the power of his might." God wants us to grow and develop into spiritual Samsons for Jesus.

We ought never be content to be weak Christians. We ought to want to be strong. In 3 John we read, "Beloved, I wish above all things that thou mayest prosper and be in health, even as thy soul prospereth." John is saying, "I am praying that your physical body will be as strong as your soul is."

What if that prayer were answered in your life? What if you left the chair where you are sitting as strong, and only as strong, in body as you are in soul? Why, some of you would have to be carried out of your home on a stretcher. Some of you are big, strong, husky, healthy people physically, yet spiritually you are weaklings. You are so susceptible to disease, spiritual disease. You are a pushover for the devil because you have never gained strength in your Christian life. That is why you give in to temptation. You are a pushover, a sissy Christian; you have never really grown.

B. Secret

Second, John says, "The word of God abideth in you" (1 John 2:14). That is the secret of growth. The word *abideth* means to "come to live." The word of God comes to live in you. When you begin to get a grip on God's word, God's word begins to get a grip on you. All mature Christians are "Bible Christians." Show me a person who has power with God, and I will show you a person who is committed to the consistent reading of the word of God.

What you need to do is begin a soul-building program. You need to stretch your spiritual muscles by daily reading the word of God. If you have to miss anything in the morning, miss your breakfast but not your Bible. Begin your day reading a portion of God's word. Let the word of God abide in you; that is the secret.

C. Success

Third, "And ye have overcome the wicked one" (1 John 2:14). John is talking here about success over the devil. The devil wants to keep you a spiritual weakling.

There are two words for "wicked" in the New Testament. One word has to do with those people who are content to go on down to degradation by themselves. But the word used here is *poneros*, from which we get the word *pornography*. It refers to those who are not content to go down the drain by themselves. They want to pull someone else down with them. John calls the devil "the wicked one," the pornographic one. In other words, the devil is not content to go to the pit by himself. The devil wants to get your life and pull you down too.

Spiritual strength, spiritual success, is conquering the wicked one. How do you do it? Let the word of God abide in you.

One of the most fascinating stories in the Bible is the story of Jesus in the garden of temptation (Matthew 4:1–11). Jesus had gone for forty days and forty nights without eating anything, and at the very weakest moment the devil came to tempt him. We know, of course, that Jesus Christ has all power, and in an instant he could have blasted the devil into oblivion. It is as if the Lord Jesus Christ looked the devil in the eye and said, "Old devil, I have all authority and all power over you, but in order to illustrate to God's children through the ages how they can have victory over you, I am going to meet you as a man. I am going to meet you in my human nature and show how it is possible to have power over you."

When the devil brought his first temptation to Jesus, Jesus reached into his heart where the word was abiding and said, "It is written, Man shall not live by bread alone, but by every word that proceedeth out of the mouth of God."

The devil threw his next temptation at him and said, "All right, if you are the Son of God, cast yourself down off the temple." Jesus reached in where the word of God was abiding and said, "It is written again, Thou shalt not tempt the Lord thy God."

The third time the devil made his attack on the Lord Jesus he said, "If you are the Son of God, fall down before me and worship me." Jesus dipped into his heart where the word of God was abiding and said, "It is written, Thou shalt worship the Lord thy God, and him only shalt thou serve." The Bible says, "Then the devil leaveth him." He was absolutely victorious over the devil.

As a Christian you can have daily victory over the devil as you let the word of God abide in you.

III. Spiritual Maturity

The word *fathers* refers to spiritual maturity. What does John say about them? He says it in verse 13 and again in verse 14. "I have written unto you, fathers, because ye have known him that is from the beginning." The words "that is" are not in the original text. "Ye have known him from the beginning." He is saying, "You have known the Lord for a long time." One of the characteristics of spiritual maturity is that you have grown in your knowledge of the Lord. Do you know more about God than you used to know? Do you know more about Jesus than when you were first saved? You ought to. The apostle Paul said in Philippians 3:10, "That I may know him, and the power of his resurrection, and the fellowship of his sufferings, being made conformable unto his death." Paul wanted to grow in his knowledge of the Lord. Spiritual maturity means you grow in your knowledge of God.

In 1 Corinthians 4:14–16 we see three things a parent is capable of doing. Paul is talking to the Corinthian believers. "For though ye have ten thousand instructors in Christ [you have a lot of folks who teach you about Jesus], yet have ye not many fathers." How many physical fathers do you have? One. How many spiritual fathers? One. Think of the man or woman or young person who led you to Jesus Christ. That person is your spiritual parent. A "father in the Lord" is capable of three things.

A. Procreation

First, he is capable of procreation. He can reproduce himself. A person is not spiritually mature until he is a spiritual father. He is not spiritually full grown until he has reproduced himself and has brought another child into the family of God. Are you a spiritual parent? Paul called Timothy "my own son in the faith." Paul told the Philippian believers, "I have no man likeminded . . . as a son with the father, he hath served with me in the gospel" (Philippians 2:20–22). Paul was Timothy's spiritual father. Timothy was Paul's spiritual son.

I have some spiritual sons who are older than I am chronologically, but younger than I am in the Lord. In fact, I am a granddaddy! I am even a great-granddaddy. I have spiritual children. I have led people to the Lord and they in turn have led someone else to the Lord and they became my grandchildren spiritually. Then that one in turn led someone else to the Lord. That is my great-grandchild.

That is what God wants you to do. That is why God saved you. One purpose of life is to reproduce itself. We ought never to be content merely to be a Christian; but our desire, our burning passion, ought to be to win other people to Jesus Christ.

B. Confrontation

A father is also capable of confrontation. In 1 Corinthians 4:14 Paul said, "I write not these things to shame you, but as my beloved sons I warn you." The word *warn* means "to speak to the heart of." It has the idea of confronting a human heart with the word of God. That is one of the things a father does with his children. He confronts their behavior with the truth. When my children do wrong I confront them with the authority of the truth. A spiritual parent is responsible to confront those whom he or she has won to Jesus Christ, to lead and guide them, to speak the truth in love and help them to grow.

C. Illustration

A father is capable of illustration. "Wherefore I beseech you, be ye followers of me" (1 Corinthians 4:16). A father has the wonderful opportunity of providing for his children an illustration of what life really ought to be.

The second church I served was a little church outside the county seat town where I was brought up. There was a deacon there who often told the story of his conversion. He was not a Christian; he had never come to Christ; he had never felt the need of Jesus. But one day he was walking out behind the house and he saw his oldest boy, just old enough to begin to follow his daddy everywhere he went. He noticed that as he was walking, taking rather long strides, the little fellow behind him was trying his best to put his little feet in the imprints of his daddy's big feet. Like a light it hit his soul, "Where are your steps leading that boy?" God used that thought to bring conviction to his soul and he came to the Lord Jesus Christ. He had suddenly realized that his life was an illustration.

> You're writing a gospel, a chapter each day.
> By deeds that you do, by words that you say.
> Others read what you write, whether faithless or true.
> Say, what is the gospel according to you?

6

Worldliness
1 John 2:15–17

I. THE MEANING OF THE WORLD
  A. What It Is Not
  B. What It Is
II. THE METHODS OF THE WORLD
  A. The Purpose of the World
  B. The Pressure of the World
III. THE MASTERY OF THE WORLD
  A. The Passing Nature of the World
  B. The Permanent Nature of the Will of God

SOON AFTER A PERSON BECOMES A CHRISTIAN HE OR SHE DISCOVERS THAT being a Christian is not a bed of roses. Rather, it is quite a battle. The Christian life is a struggle against formidable enemies. A child of God has three great foes: first, an external enemy, the world; second, an internal enemy, the flesh; third, an infernal enemy, the devil. First, let us look at what the Bible says about the world.

John warns us that we are not to love the world; if we love the world, the love of the Father is not in us. John is saying, "It is impossible for you to love two exact opposites at the same time." Jesus put it like this: "No man can serve two masters: for either he will hate the one, and love the other; or else he will hold to the one, and despise the other. Ye cannot serve God and mammon" (Matthew 6:24). We are exhorted by the word of God not to love this world.

Worldliness is one of the problems of the modern church. It plagues our churches and keeps them from having the power of God. It robs us of our spiritual effectiveness; it ruins our witness for the Lord.

To speak of a worldly Christian is a misnomer. Billy Sunday the evangelist was correct when he said, "It makes no more sense to talk about a worldly Christian than to talk about a heavenly devil." I am convinced that many of those we call worldly Christians are not actually Christians at all. If I see a bird that looks like a duck and quacks like a duck and waddles like a duck and eats like a duck, then I get the idea that such a bird probably is a duck. If I see a person who acts like the world and lives like the world and loves the world and is part of the world, then I am driven to certain inevitable conclusions.

From the word of God, we can understand what worldliness is. Many Christians who are worldly would not be worldly if they knew what the world is, if they knew what the world is doing to them, how the world operates and where the world is going.

I. The Meaning of the World

What does John mean when he says, "Love not the world, neither the things that are in the world" (1 John 2:15)?

A. What It Is Not

When John talks about the world, he does not mean the world of nature—not the flowers and trees, the mountains and seas, which are part of the world of nature. Acts 17:24 says, "God . . . made the world and all things therein." When the Bible tells you not to love this world it does not mean the world of physical nature. There is still beauty in this fallen creation, enough to take away the breath and to thrill the hearts of those who see it. In fact, when you come to know Jesus as your Savior and look at this world through converted eyes, you are able to appreciate the beauty of the world and the beauty of nature around you in a better way. It all points to our heavenly Father who made it for us to enjoy. Scripture says in the book of 1 Timothy that he gave us richly all things to enjoy.

Neither does John mean the world of humanity when he speaks like this. The Bible says in John 3:16, "For God so loved the world, that he gave his only begotten Son, that whosoever believeth in him should not perish, but have everlasting life." Jesus loved the world of humanity. God loved it and sent his Son into the world to die on the cross for the sins of the world. In telling us not to love the world, John does not mean the world of lost humanity. We too ought to love the world of lost sinners. Someone said, "If we loved the world as God loves it, we would not love the world as we ought not to love it."

B. What It Is

The word for "world" used here is *kosmos*, from which we get "cosmopolitan" and "cosmic." The word *kosmos* is taken from a verb that means "to order," "to arrange," or "to put in the proper condition."

We use the word in this way many times. We talk about the world of sports, meaning a system of ideas and activities of people who are involved in sports. We talk about the world of politics, meaning an attitude, a system, and the activities of people who are involved in politics. When the Bible tells us, "Love not the world," it is talking about an arrangement of things or a system that is opposed to God.

The Bible says a great deal about this world. It tells us that this world has a temporary ruler. In 2 Corinthians 4:4 we read, "The god of this world hath blinded the minds of them which believe not." John 12:31 says, "Now is the judgment of this world: now shall the prince of this world be cast out." And 1 John 5:19 says, "We know that we are of God, and the whole world lieth in wickedness." This world has a ruler and the world is in the lap of the wicked one.

We are also told that this world has its children. Jesus said, "The children of this world are in their generation wiser than the children of light" (Luke 16:8). There are two families in existence: the family of God (those who belong to the heavenly world, those who belong to the heavenly city), and those who belong to this world. This is the only world they have any awareness of.

The Bible also tells us in 1 Corinthians 2:6, 12 that this world has a spirit. It talks about the "spirit of this world" and the "wisdom of this world." This world does have a kind of wisdom. Yet it is a warped, twisted, perverted wisdom.

This world is corrupt through its lust (2 Peter 1:4). It seeks to hinder the children of God from being what they ought to be.

This world put Jesus Christ on the cross. Jesus said in John 15:19, "If ye were of the world, the world would love his own: but because ye are not of the world, but I have chosen you out of the world, therefore the world hateth you." This world is not a friend to God's children; it is not a friend to help us on to God. It is our enemy, our antagonist. The world system wants to keep us away from God and rob us of the blessings that God has in store for us.

With that kind of definition of the world, a system of things opposed to God, then what is worldliness?

I am not going to name specific things for several reasons. Number one, it would take me practically all day to do it if I were going to name everything that is worldly. Number two, if I did name some things, people would want to argue with me— because opinions differ about what constitutes worldliness. In some sections of our country things are considered worldly by some Christians and other things are not. I read the other day, for instance, that in Finland it is considered worldly to whistle. I doubt that many of you feel it is worldly to whistle.

Worldliness is anything that keeps you from loving God as you ought to love him, and from doing the will of God as you ought to do it. It is anything that comes between you and God and keeps you from living the Christian life to the fullest. If there is anything in your life about which you have a question, anything you are doing that you really do not feel at ease before God about, then you ought to quit it. A pretty good axiom for the child of God is this: "If in doubt, don't!" If it is questionable, then leave it off.

II. The Methods of the World

How does the world operate? What are the methods the world uses to try to get us to be like it?

In John 17 we see what Jesus said about our relationship to the world. Here we have his great high priestly prayer, really the Lord's prayer. (When Jesus taught us to pray, "Our Father which art in heaven, . . ." that was not the Lord's prayer. That is the model prayer or the disciples' prayer.)

We need to know four things about our relationship to this world. Jesus says, "I have manifested thy name unto the men which thou gavest me out of the world" (John 17:6). If you are saved, you have been saved out of this world system. You do not belong to this world system anymore. Galatians 1:4 says that Christ died for us "that he might deliver us [rescue us] from this present evil world."

Jesus says, "And now I am no more in the world, but these are in the world" (John 17:11). All of us also need to know that we are still in this world. We have to live in this world's houses, trade in its businesses, work in its factories. Being saved does not take us out of this world physically.

Jesus says, "I have given them thy word; and the world hath hated them, because they are not of the world, even as I am not of the world" (John 17:14). We are saved out of the world, we are still in the world, and we are not of the world. We are still here and yet we really do not belong here.

Jesus says, "As thou hast sent me into the world, even so have I also sent them into the world" (John 17:18). We are in it, we are not of it, and yet he has sent us into this world. We are not in this world to condemn it, nor to condone it, but to confront it with the claims of the Lord Jesus Christ.

If you will keep that in mind, you will understand better the methods of the world. What the world wants is to cause you not only to be in the world, but to be of the world. It wants you to go along with the world and become indistinguishable from the rest of its people.

A. The Purpose of the World

The world wants to displace the love of God in your heart and replace it with love for this world. The process the world uses is subtle.

First, it will start by trying to get you to be friendly with this world. It will approach you like this, "You know you are here, so you might as well go along and take the course of least resistance. After all, you don't want to be a Holy Joe, an old fuddy-duddy, a stick-in-the-mud; you don't want to be different. Just be friends with this world."

In James 4:4 God says, "Ye adulterers and adulteresses, know ye not that the friendship of the world is enmity with God? whosoever therefore will be a friend of the world is the enemy of God." Friendship with the world is spiritual adultery. Flirting with the world is unfaithfulness to the Lord Jesus Christ. Be careful how friendly you become with this world. The next step after friendliness is courtship, and the next step after courtship is engagement, and the next step after engagement is marriage.

Second, after you start getting friendly with the world, you get tainted by it. James 1:27 says, "Pure religion and undefiled before God and the Father is this, To visit the fatherless and widows in their affliction, and to keep himself unspotted from the world." You are living in a dirty world, a smutty, rotten, grimy world. If you get too friendly with the world, the dirt of the world will surely get on you. You go out into the world, work in its factories and offices, and you hear the filthy language and obscene jokes. When you get home you feel as if you need a bath, not only physically, but also mentally and spiritually. You cannot get close to the world and not get tainted by it.

The Bible warns us about being no different from the world. "Be not conformed to this world" (Romans 12:2). J. B. Phillips puts it this way: "Do not let the world squeeze you into its mold." I like that. In other words, this world has a mold. This world wants to turn out carbon copies that think as it thinks, act as it acts, do as it does, go where it goes, have the same standard it has. If you are friends of the world, next you will get conformed to this world. There will not be a bit of difference between you and any other worldly person.

One of the tragedies of Christians is that they are so conformed to the standards of this world. Anything the world does, the average Christian does. It does not matter how lowdown the world gets, some Christians want to be just exactly like it. We do not want to be weirdos.

The way some Christians live is appalling, a disgrace to God. Our public immodesty is a disgrace. You cannot tell the differ-

ence between saved people and lost people by the way they
dress, the way they act, and the places of amusement they go to.

First Corinthians 11:32 warns that you will be "condemned
with this world." That does not mean you will lose your salvation. It means you will lose your usefulness. You will lose your
testimony for the Lord.

It happened to Demas. In 2 Timothy 4:10 the Bible says about
Demas, "For Demas hath forsaken me, having loved this present world." I do not think Demas became an alcoholic; I do not
think he went off into deep sin. Demas had the experience a lot
of Christians have. He loved the Lord, but he started letting
some of the things of the world creep into his life and replace
his love for the Lord. He started putting other activities between himself and his service for Jesus. He began to neglect his
Bible, his prayer life. He became unfaithful to the services, and
dropped off in his visitation, and after a while he became so
wrapped up in material things that he left Paul and said, "I am
going back home and I am going to spend my life looking out
for Number One—me!"

It happened to Lot. You would never know that Lot was a believer unless you read it in the New Testament. Yet the Bible
says that Lot was a righteous man. Lot was a righteous man living in a tent. One day he decided to pitch his tent toward
Sodom. He compromised just a little. He moved to the border
and engaged in borderline sin. He was living out there on the
edge of town and his children were going to "Sodom High" and
his wife was a member of the "Sodom aerobics club." Finally,
because it got increasingly inconvenient to be driving back and
forth so much, he and his family moved into Sodom.

Lot was friends with the world, he got spotted by the world,
and the next thing you read about him he is living in Sodom,
conformed to this world. He nearly lost his life down in Sodom
and he had become so attached to the world that only an angel
of God could get him out.

A man starts off living for the Lord, close to the Lord, on fire
for God. Then he gets busy making money. He moves up in the
political sphere. He gets busy doing other things and neglects
God's house, neglects his prayer life. Many a man would give
everything he possesses to have the joy and closeness with Jesus

he used to have and have his family united once again. That is
what this world will do to you.

B. The Pressure of the World

This world puts pressure on us in three ways: first, through
"the lust of the flesh" (1 John 2:16), the appeal to the body. There
is nothing wrong with the body. *Lust* means "desires, the crav-
ings, the longings of the body." Though the body itself is not sinful, we have a fallen nature that makes an improper appeal to
the natural desires of our body. The world wants to cause us to
try to satisfy those normal desires in abnormal ways.

The desire for food is normal, but when we use that desire for
food to eat too much and abuse our body, we are worldly. We are
guilty of "lust of the flesh."

There is not a thing wrong with money. The Bible does not
say that money is evil. We must have money to live. But the
Bible says, "The love of money is the root of all evil." Nothing is
wrong with getting money, but the world takes a normal desire
and wants us to use unjust methods of getting it.

Sex is not wrong. The book of Hebrews says that the marriage
bed is undefiled and marriage should be honored by all. God
created sex, and within proper boundaries it is good, beautiful,
and deeply spiritual. But the devil wants us to try to satisfy this
normal desire in improper ways. When we do, we ruin it. We
make it something dirty and ugly and shameful.

The devil also appeals to the mind, "the lust of the eyes." Because much of what we think comes through the eye-gate, we
ought to be careful what we watch with our eyes. One of the
greatest hindrances in the Christian home is television. Something is wrong when Christian people will sit in their
livingroom and watch things they would not have dared to have
gone to a movie to see a few years ago; further, they allow their
children to hear profane and vulgar language they would not
have allowed in their home a few years ago. The pictures the
devil puts on television in front of our eyes are controlled pictures. He wants us to see just exactly what he wants us to see,
and he never lets us see the true picture.

I ride up and down the roads of our country and see the devil's pictures. I see all of the beauty and enticements and every-

thing the devil offers. And I say in my soul, "Devil, why don't you turn the billboard around and show the true picture? Why don't you show it the way it really is?"

"The lust of the eyes." Watch what you put in your mind through your eyes. That is what happened to Achan. God said to destroy Jericho and not let a thing survive. Achan saw a Babylonian garment, shekels of silver, and a wedge of gold. He coveted them in his heart and took them. Many Christians have lost their testimony through "the lust of the eyes."

Finally, the devil appeals to the spirit: "the pride of life." The word *pride* means "the empty display of life." It means the vain boasting of one's lifestyle. It means living in such a way as to impress other people. It means building bigger and better houses and having bigger and better cars, and loving clothes—all for the sake of showing off. It means the display of a fancy lifestyle so people will think you are something.

Some folks get into financial messes by buying things they don't need. Isn't the average young couple up to their ears in debt? The first thing they want to do is have a well-furnished apartment. Next they buy a color television set. Then they buy a sports car.

It does not matter whether you can pay for these things or not. You must have all of them because that is what this world expects you to have and you are trying to keep up.

Sometimes people get worldly spiritually. Does that sound like a contradiction? Some people display their spirituality in such a way that it is worldly. Some try to make folks think they are more spiritual than they actually are. I get suspicious of people who are always parading their holiness, always showing you how good they are, how Christian they are, how spiritual. If you are spiritual, if you are hooked up right with God, you do not have to wear a sign. Folks will know you are right with God. A lot of what goes on in the name of religion is just as worldly as it can be because it is rooted in "the pride of life" and it appeals to the flesh.

III. The Mastery of the World

How do we conquer the world? "The world passeth away, and

the lust thereof: but he that doeth the will of God abideth forever" (1 John 2:17).

A. The Passing Nature of the World

This world is passing away. This world is a goner. Jesus said
that heaven and earth shall pass away. First Corinthians 7:31
says, "The fashion of this world passeth away." This whole thing
is going to crumble one of these days. Look at these massive
buildings that cost fortunes to erect. One of these days those
buildings are going to come crashing to the ground. Look at the
amusement centers people go to, to try to dull their senses and
keep them away from God. One of these days "the elements
shall melt with fervent heat" (2 Peter 3:10). This world of ours is
going to go out of existence.

That is why this world cannot permanently satisfy anyone; it
is not lasting. That is why drink will not satisfy you. It will not
last. That is why drugs will not satisfy you. You move from
marijuana to cocaine and cocaine to heroin and it will finally
kill you. This world's pleasures are fading. So we had better get
hold of something more enduring than what this world has to
offer. If we anchor our life in this world, we have anchored it to a
floating island and we too will pass away.

Do not put your roots down in this world; do not put your
hopes in this world; do not fall in love with this world. It is not
worth it.

B. The Permanent Nature of the Will of God

We will never put this world beneath us until we have seen a
better world above. Consider the Old Testament saints. They
were willing to live in tents in this world. Why? They "were
looking for a city whose builder and maker is God" (Hebrews
11:10). They had discovered that there was something better
than houses and lands and material things. They had fallen out
of love with this world and in love with the will of God, doing
the things of God.

One day when I was a little boy I was playing marbles. I loved
to play marbles. My ambition was to be the world's champion
marble player. I was playing marbles one day and some big boys

came by who said, "Hey, kid. Can you hit a baseball?" I answered, "Why of course I can hit a baseball!" They said, "Well,
we need one more on our side. Come on!" I emptied my pocket
of marbles, I left to play baseball with the big boys, and I never
went back to a marble game again. I had found something
better.

When you discover that the will of God is better, that loving
God is more precious than anything this world has to offer, you
will not mind giving up the world. You will not hate giving it
up. No, when you really start doing the will of God you discover pleasures that are lasting. The Bible says there are
"pleasures of sin for a season," but "at thy right hand there are
pleasures for evermore."

Would you go all the way with Jesus? Our young people sing a
little song that I like. I hope they mean it and I hope you mean it.
"I have decided to follow Jesus. The world behind me, the cross
before me. No turning back, no turning back."

If you are lost, I do not blame you for being worldly. I do not
blame you for getting all you can out of this world, because
this is the only world you are ever going to have. If you are
lost, all the heaven you will ever get you are going to get on
this earth and then it is gone forever. I want to introduce you
to a better world.

7

Those Who Go Away
1 John 2:18–27

I. THEY DENY THE CHRIST
   A. The Antichrist
   B. The Antichrists
II. THEY DESERT THE CHURCH
   A. Physical Desertion
   B. Moral Desertion
   C. Intellectual Desertion
III. THEY DECEIVE THE CHRISTIAN
   A. Confuse the Christian
   B. Convert the Christian

JOHN IS VERY MUCH CONCERNED FOR THE SPIRITUAL GROWTH AND DEVELOP-ment of Christians. First John 2:14 gives his words about the fathers in the Lord, those who are spiritually mature. He says to them, "Ye have known him that is from the beginning." To the young he says, "Ye are strong, and the word of God abideth in you, and ye have overcome the wicked one." Finally, he speaks to the little children, those who are immature, baby Christians, just beginning to grow in the Lord.

It is important for children to know many things, including how to tell time. You have to teach little children how to tell time. In 1 John 2:18 the apostle says, "Little children, it is the last time." John is saying to these young children in the Lord that they are living in the last time. If John said that about his day, I wonder what he would have to say about our day.

Have you heard the story about the farmer who went to bed one night and something went wrong with his clock? It chimed fourteen times. He jumped up and said to his wife, "Get up, Nellie, it is later than it has ever been before!" I think John would say that if he were alive today, that we surely are in the last time.

There is a sense in which the last time began in the days of John and has been growing in intensity until now. We have been in the last time since the days of the Lord Jesus. The Bible indicates that toward the close of the age there will be latter days of increased difficulty and turmoil. In 2 Timothy 3:1 the Bible says, "This know also, that in the last days perilous times shall come." Again in 1 Timothy 4:1 we are told, "Now the Spirit speaketh expressly, that in the latter times some shall depart from the faith." I believe we are living in the last days of the last time.

Many things will characterize those last days. Among them will be the fact that some who profess to belong to the church of the Lord Jesus Christ will turn and go away. "In the latter times some shall depart from the faith." Our Lord said there would be in those days the wheat, which represents the genuine and the true, and the tares, which represent the imitation and the false.

This is what John tries to get across to young Christians in these verses. Notice the sharp contrast in verse 19 between "they" and "us." The original says "they" six times and five times it says "us." John is talking about those who go away and those of us who remain. Three crucial things are said about those who go away.

I. THEY DENY THE CHRIST

Verses 18, 22–23 tell us that those who go away deny the Christ.

A. The Antichrist

John says it will be characteristic in those days that the antichrist will come and that there will also be antichrists (plural) in the world. "Ye have heard that antichrist shall come." In John

5:43 Jesus said, "I am come in my Father's name, and ye receive me not: if another shall come in his own name, him ye will receive." Jesus predicted that there would come a final personality of evil. He would come in his own name and, though people would reject God's Christ, they would accept and receive the devil's antichrist.

The apostle Paul also had something to say about this antichrist, this satanic superman who would make his appearance just before the return of the Lord. In 2 Thessalonians 2:3 we read, "Let no man deceive you by any means: for that day shall not come, except there come a falling away first, and that man of sin be revealed, the son of perdition." Paul is clearly predicting the arrival of that final man, that man who will be the antichrist.

When Jesus came into this world, the devil offered him all the kingdoms of this world if he would fall down and worship him. Jesus said, "Depart from me, Satan," and refused the offer of the devil. In the latter days the devil will make this same offer to a man. That man will take the devil up on the offer, and the devil will give to him the kingdoms of this world. He will be the final world ruler who will represent the devil upon the earth.

B. The Antichrists

In the meantime many antichrists will be in existence. They were in existence in the days of John, and there are antichrists and antichrist systems in our day. In 1 John 4:1 we read, "Beloved, believe not every spirit, but try the spirits whether they are of God: because many false prophets are gone out into the world."

First John 4:3 continues, "And every spirit that confesseth not that Jesus Christ is come in the flesh is not of God: and this is that spirit of antichrist, whereof ye have heard that it should come; and even now already is it in the world." The key to whether a doctrine is Christian is this: What does it believe about Christ? If it denies that Christ shed his blood on the cross for the atonement of the sins of the world, then that system or that teacher is an antichrist in nature.

The only way we will ever get to God is through the Lord Jesus Christ. Jesus said that he that honors not the Son honors not the

Father, but he that honors the Father honors the Son also. In John 14:6 Jesus said, "I am the way, the truth, and the life: no man cometh unto the Father, but by me." The first characteristic of those who go away is that they deny the Christ.

II. They Desert the Church

Characteristic number two is found in 1 John 2:19. They desert the church. "They went out from us, but they were not of us; for if they had been of us, they would no doubt have continued with us." Desertion of the church can take at least three forms.

A. Physical Desertion

First, there may be physical desertion: those who have affiliated themselves with the church yet they do not come any more.

What would happen if every person who belonged to the church came on a particular Sunday? Well, the pastor might have a heart attack first of all! A few years ago a woman walked into a store after Easter Sunday and said to someone who was a member of a church in that town, "I wish you folks who go to church regularly would stay home on Easter so we who come on Easter could get a seat!"

John said, "There will be those who will go out from us because they are not of us." Church membership does not mean that you are born into the family of God. Physical union with the church does not mean that you have real, vital, spiritual union with the family of God.

There are those who may appear to be saved yet in reality are not. I do not think anybody suspected Judas. In fact when Jesus said, "There is one in our midst who is going to betray me," the disciples all began to say "Is it I?" Judas was a good actor. He was part of them, but he was not one of them. He went out from them that it might be manifest that he was not of them.

We face the real possibility that those who once came to the house of God, and now do not, have never truly been born of the Spirit of God. When they go out they show what they are in their heart; they show what they actually were all the time.

Second Peter 2:22 says, "But it is happened unto them according to the true proverb, The dog is turned to his own vomit again; and the sow that was washed to her wallowing in the mire."

Do you get the picture? A hog is just a hog and you will never make anything out of it but a hog. You can put a hog in the livingroom, put a little red ribbon around its neck and curl its tail, and it can be just the prettiest little thing you ever saw. But give it an opportunity and it will head for the hog pen and jump right into the mud. It was a hog all along. It does not matter how you clean it up, it is still a hog, and the first chance it gets it will manifest to the world that it is a hog.

B. Moral Desertion

Also, there is moral desertion: Some lead their lives apart from the discipline of the church of God and their life becomes a total contradiction to all the church of the Lord Jesus Christ stands for. It is an amazing thing to me that when moral issues come up, there are those whose names are on the rolls of churches who take their stand on the opposite side of what is right and true and good. I do not believe that people who get on Satan's side are a part of the family of God. You cannot make me believe it in a million years. Their life is a moral contradiction. The church is for purity; they are for impurity. The church stands for righteousness; they are on the side of unrighteousness. Their life is a source of embarrassment and their conduct is a burden to the people of God.

C. Intellectual Desertion

The Bible also talks about intellectual desertion from the church and this is what the Bible means when it talks about those who apostatize from the faith. These are those who profess to know the Lord and believe the doctrines of the faith for a time. Later they deny the fundamentals of the faith and yet remain in the church. They retain their membership in a church of the Christian faith while they deny the doctrines that give Christianity its distinctive flavor.

These people often are promoted to places of importance. They get into pulpits and they deny the essential doctrines of

the word of God right in the pulpit that is dedicated to promulgate those doctrines. They invade chairs of religion, and Christian people support folks who do not even believe in the
inspiration of the scriptures and the blood atonement of Jesus
Christ. They get in places of denominational leadership and
want to lead denominations away from the fundamentals of the
faith that made them great. We give all kinds of labels to these
people. We talk about the modernist Christian, the liberal
Christian. I am convinced on the basis of the study of the word
that such terminology is not within the realm of Christian
possibility.

In 2 John 9 we are told, "Whosoever transgresseth, and
abideth not in the doctrine of Christ, hath not God." I did not say
that. That is what the infallible word of God says. It says that
when you depart from the doctrine, when you deviate from the
doctrine of Christ, it is an evidence that you do not have Christ.
Some who profess to know the Lord and yet deny the essential
doctrines of the Christian faith need to have an old-fashioned
experience of grace.

I love a story Harry Ironside tells in one of his books. He says
there was a man who at one time preached the doctrines of the
Christian faith and then began to doubt them. He preached only
a social gospel. One night this preacher was getting ready to go
to bed when a knock came on his door. At the door was a little
girl who said to this preacher, "I wonder if you could come down
to my house. My mama is terribly sick."

The preacher said, "If your mama is drunk, call the police and
let them come get her."

The girl replied, "Mama is not drunk. She is dying and she
told me to get a preacher."

The man thought to himself, "I cannot go to that kind of place.
What would happen to my reputation if I went there?" So he
said, "Get the rescue mission man and let him go down there. I
cannot go."

She persisted, "But my mama said to get a real preacher and
you are the only real preacher I know. Would you please see my
mama?" So he put his clothes on and made his way down to the
place where the mother was dying.

She said to him, "O preacher, O preacher, I am dying. Can you tell me something about God? Can you tell me how to get to heaven?"

He began to think, "I have been preaching salvation by character but she does not have any. I cannot tell her that. I have been preaching salvation by reformation but there is no time for her to reform. I have been preaching salvation by culture but she does not have any time to acquire culture. What am I going to tell her?" He began to think of some of the verses his mother had taught him when he was a boy, so he quoted John 3:16 to her.

She said, "Oh, sir, do you mean God loved the world and God loves even me?"

And he said, "Well, I guess that is right." Next he quoted to her how the blood of Christ cleanses from all sin and she said, "Oh, sir, do you mean that Christ's blood will cleanse me from every sin I have ever committed?"

And he said, "Well, yes, that is right." And he thought of another verse his mother had told him when he was a boy: "Whosoever will, let him come."

And she said, "Oh, sir, does that mean that even I could come and be saved?"

And he said, "Yes, it does." You know what that preacher said? He said that night he "got her in" and, praise God, he got himself in too!

That is what we need. We need to meet Jesus. I have never known a truly born-again believer who deviated very far from the essential doctrines of the Christian faith.

III. They Deceive the Christian

Those who go away also deceive the Christian. "These things have I written unto you concerning them that seduce you" (1 John 2:26). It is often the desire of those who apostatize from the Christian faith to lead other Christians astray also. They do it in two ways.

A. Confuse the Christian

They prey on young Christians. When they find someone who has just become a Christian they immediately pounce on that young Christian and in effect begin to say, "I want to show you the true way." They try to confuse him or her about the simplicities of the Christian faith.

In 1 Timothy 4:1 the Bible gives us some of the characteristics of those who would seek to deceive young Christians. "Now the Spirit speaketh expressly, that in the latter times some shall depart from the faith, giving heed to seducing spirits, and doctrines of devils." The devil has doctrines too. Then Paul names a few of them. "Forbidding to marry"—that is one of the doctrines of the devil (1 Timothy 4:3). Do you know a group anywhere that forbids its clergy to marry? "Commanding to abstain from meats"—have you heard of any group that is overly conscious about diet? It is good to diet. I need to do a little and some of you need to do a lot but that does not have a thing in the world to do with your salvation. "Forbidding to eat meats, which God hath created to be received with thanksgiving of them which believe and know the truth"—false teachers go off on tangents. They veer away from the main points and develop other emphases.

A sweet Christian couple came to my study one Saturday and for three hours I sought to untangle their mind about the word of God. A man had come through town professing to be a Bible teacher (and every time such persons come through and claim they are the only right ones, you had better watch it). There is something wrong with the fellow who thinks he has all the answers. This man had taught them that the great tribulation was at hand. He had them about ready to sell their home, and by the way, give him all the money. Isn't that interesting? Give him all the money and get ready to go through the great tribulation. I took the word of God and tried to undo the damage and settled the confusion by showing them what God has to say in his word. Thankfully, they are now busily serving the Lord because they were not allowed to be misled by one who went away.

B. Convert the Christian

Those who go away also seek to convert young Christians. They are not interested in visiting the lost. Those who apostatize from the Christian faith are not interested in going out into the highways and byways and winning those who are lost in sin. They prey on church members. If you look at the rolls of the

major cults in America, you will discover that the majority of
their members are Baptist, Methodist, Church of God, or Pres-
byterian people who were not well grounded in the word of God
and who were converted by these cults into their false doctrines. That is exactly the way they do it. They seek to convert
young Christians to the error of their way.

What are we going to do? How can young Christians counteract the spirit of antichrist that is so prevalent? In these verses
John gives us a threefold remedy.

The first place to stay is in the church of God. "They went out
from us, . . . if they had been of us, they would no doubt have
continued with us." Stay in the church. Wherever in a community the word of God is preached in a local church, that church
is "the pillar and ground of the truth" (1 Timothy 3:15). That
makes the local church very important.

Do you say, "I am not so hot on the local church; I believe in
the church universal"? I do too, but I also believe in the church
visible and the church local. The church universal never holds
a meeting, never takes up a collection, never sends a missionary. When you study the New Testament you will see that God
puts priority on local church ministry. Other organizations
have their place and can perform needful services, but nothing
on this earth is so crucial as the ministry of the local church.
Acts 20:28 says, "Feed the church of God, which he hath purchased with his own blood." Every group that exists in opposi-
tion to or in competition with the local church is destined to die.
Find a Bible church, get in it, and stay in it. Submit yourselves to
the discipline of that Bible-believing church and you will grow
in your Christian life.

The second place you ought to stay is in the word of God.
"Let that therefore abide in you, which ye heard from the beginning" (1 John 2:24). John is talking about something you can
hear, the word of God. Abide in the word of God; stay in the
word of God. "If that which ye have heard from the beginning
shall remain in you, ye also shall continue in the Son, and in
the Father."

Jesus makes an interesting statement about the word of God.
In John 17:17 he says, "Thy word is truth." Notice he does not
say, "Thy word is true." Yes, it is true; the Bible is true, of course.
But Jesus says, "Thy word is truth." *Truth* is what makes every-

thing else true. In 1 Peter 2 the Bible says, "Unto you . . . which believe he [Jesus] is precious." But literally it is, "He is the preciousness." *Preciousness* is what makes everything else precious. To say that the Word of God is truth means that the Bible makes everything else true. I do not care if Dr. Bottlestopper or Professor Dry-As-Dust says it, if it does not agree with the word of God it is not true. And if it is not true, it is a lie. The Bible is truth. Get in it; study it; stay in it.

First Thessalonians 2:13 says, "For this cause also thank we God without ceasing, because, when ye received the word of God which ye heard of us, ye received it not as the word of men, but as it is in truth, the word of God, which effectually worketh also in you that believe."

Do you appreciate the Bible? Men and women have given their life in order to give you a copy of the Bible in your own language. Do you appropriate the Bible? It is not enough just to read it; you have to let the Bible influence your daily life. You have to appropriate its truths in your home life, social life, business life.

The third place you ought to stay is in the Spirit of God. First John 2:20 says, "But ye have an unction from the Holy One, and ye know all things." The word *unction* is translated "anointing" in verse 27. "You have an anointing from the Holy One." The word *anointing* or *unction* means "to anoint with oil." It is a reference to an Old Testament ceremony in which a prophet, priest, or king was anointed with oil and thereby set apart for particular service. We are told that Jesus was anointed by God the Father. Jesus said, "The Spirit of the Lord is upon me because he hath anointed me to preach the gospel to the poor." Jesus anoints every believer at salvation.

Dr. Lewis Sperry Chafer in his *Systematic Theology* says that when you are saved at least thirty-three things happen to you. When I got saved I did not know so much had happened to me! When you are saved he establishes you. "Now he which stablishes us with you in Christ. . . ." (2 Corinthians 1:21). That is really in the past tense. He established you.

"Who hath also sealed us . . ." (2 Corinthians 1:22). When God saves you, you are sealed—signed, sealed, and delivered. You are just as good as in heaven. He has given us the earnest of the Spirit as the down payment; that means there is more to follow.

"And [he] hath anointed us . . ." (2 Corinthians 1:21). When you are saved, God gives you the anointing of the Holy Spirit. We do not pray for the Spirit's anointing in the sense that we pray for what we get in salvation—although sometimes we pray for a fresh anointing, that God will give us a new infilling of his power. The fervent prayer of my heart is that God will give me a fresh anointing, enabling me to preach in the power of the Holy Spirit.

Every believer has an anointing and "you know all things." That does not mean you know all things about mathematics. Kids, do not go to school next week and say, "The preacher said I know all things; I am not going to study. I know all things about math." That is not what it is saying. It does not mean you know all things about philosophy; it does not mean you know all things about chemistry. It means that when the Holy Spirit of God is in your heart you have the ability to detect error. The Spirit of God, who is truth, is within you and when you as a Spirit-indwelt believer hear a lie, the Holy Spirit of God lets you know it.

I went to a liberal college. I sat for four years under some liberal men who did not believe that the Bible was the word of God. They were far smarter than I would ever profess to be. They were intelligent men, but they did not accept the Bible as the infallible word of God. If I did not believe the Bible, do you think I would be here pouring my life out preaching? Would I take a salary from people who believe the Bible if I did not believe it myself? I would have enough intellectual honesty to get out of the ministry. I would hear those liberal men say, "It does not mean this and it does not mean this and it does not mean this." As I sat there in class, down inside it was just like an alarm clock going off.

You see, God puts an alarm system in you, if you are saved. A missionary to the Indians in America took a converted Indian chief to Los Angeles. They were walking down the street and a false teacher was standing on the corner with a Bible, putting out false doctrine. The missionary was afraid that the convert would see the Bible and think what the man was saying was true. They stood there for a moment and listened. After they went by, the missionary said, "What did you think about that man who spoke?" The Indian replied, "I don't know what it was, but all the time he was talking something inside me was saying, 'Liar, liar, liar.'" That something was someone, the Holy Spirit, detecting error. Young people, don't ever be intimidated when you get in a classroom and they tell you the devil's lies and that spirit of antichrist makes it appear you are a fool if you do not believe what is being taught. Listen to the inner witness of the Holy Spirit. "You have an anointing and you know all things."

The Spirit not only detects error but he teaches truth. "But the anointing which ye have received of him abideth in you" (1 John 2:27). You have a built-in Bible teacher. Sometimes when you study a book you may think, "I wish I could talk to the man who wrote this so he could clarify what he means." When you read the Bible you have the author of that Bible down in your heart to interpret what it says. He abides in you and you need not let any man teach you.

This does not deny the New Testament office of teaching. No, Roman 12 makes clear that some persons have the gift of teaching. Ephesians 4:11 says that the Lord gives to the church pastors and teachers. God teaches me through others. I read books and listen to sermons and I get everything I can from them. Yes, we can learn from others, but John is saying that when a Bible teacher is teaching the word of God, we ought to hear far more than what the Bible teacher says. The Holy Spirit of God ought to be ministering and teaching our heart at the same time.

I have a great time when I hear a Bible teacher. As I sit there and listen, something else is going on. The Holy Spirit is teaching me. The Bible teacher mentions this truth right here and the Spirit of God will take that and lead me off over there and I see this and I see that. Such a thought process is the real amplified Bible. It just gets bigger and bigger and then I have a spiritual feast. I have an anointing and I need not that any mere man teach me.

"The same anointing teacheth you of all things." If you will let him, the Holy Spirit will teach you everything you need to know to be the kind of Christian you ought to be. Stay in the church of God, in the word of God, and in the Spirit of God.

8

How Do You Want to Meet Him?
1 John 2:28–29

I. ABIDE
   A. The Church of God
   B. The Word of God
   C. The Spirit of God
II. APPEAR
   A. Looking
   B. Loving
   C. Living
III. ASHAMED
   A. Appear
   B. Acceptable
   C. Ashamed

THE LAST TWO VERSES OF 1 JOHN 2 SERVE AS A BRIDGE BETWEEN THE TWO main themes of the book. In the first two chapters John deals with fellowship, or how to walk daily with God. In chapters 3 through 5 he deals with sonship, or being born of God. Verse 28 is a climactic or summary verse, which gathers together what he has been trying to say about fellowship with God. Verse 29 introduces us to the theme of being born of God.

First John 2:28 has an interesting sequence of words about our relationship to God and our fellowship with him.

I. ABIDE

The first word is *abide.* "And now, little children, abide in him." This is essential if we are going to be prepared to meet the Lord when he comes. The word *abide* is the key word in the first two chapters of 1 John. Eleven times in the second chapter alone he has used this word, which has to do not with salvation, but with fellowship with God, our walking close to the Lord daily. Some things are essential if we are going to have fellowship with God on a daily basis.

A. The Church of God

To abide in Jesus Christ is to abide in the church of God. Fellowship with God is essential if we are going to be what God wants us to be, and we cannot be in fellowship with God unless we abide in the church of God.

First Timothy 3:15, as has been noted, says that the church is the pillar and ground of the truth. God has deposited his truth in local congregations of believers. If we are going to have fellowship with God, we have to stay in a church where the truth is presented and where the word of God is set forth.

As a Christian you have certain responsibilities to the church of the Lord.

First, you owe your church your presence. I do believe in the concept of the universal and invisible church. Some people, however, have a concept of the invisible church that causes them to be invisible on Sunday morning, Sunday night, and Wednesday night. The Bible teaches us that it is important for God's people to give their church their presence. Your presence at a service says that you are committed to what is going on in that church and that you believe in what the church is trying to do. Hebrews 10:25 says, "Not forsaking the assembling of ourselves together, as the manner of some is: but exhorting one another: and so much the more, as ye see the day approaching."

Second, you owe your church your prayers. You ought to pray daily for the fellowship to which you belong. You ought to pray daily for its pastor or elders, for its staff, and for its activities and ministries.

Third, you owe your church your participation. You ought to be involved in everything your church is doing. I believe that Christians ought to be totally involved in every activity of their church. I think you ought to be in Sunday school on Sunday morning without fail unless providentially hindered. You ought to be in the worship services Sunday morning and Sunday night. You ought to come to the church training and to the prayer meeting and engage yourself in the visitation ministry of the church. To abide in Jesus means we are to abide in the church of God.

B. The Word of God

To abide in Jesus means also to abide in the word of God. As we maintain daily Bible study time we stay in fellowship with God and we grow in our Christian faith. You have at least three responsibilities in relation to the word of God.

First, you owe it to yourself to study the word of God. In Acts 17:11 we are told about the Berean Christians. Scripture says concerning them: "These were more noble than those in Thessalonica, in that they received the word with all readiness of mind, and searched the scriptures daily, whether those things were so." You owe it to yourself to study the word of God daily, diligently, and discerningly. Jesus said in John 5:39, "Search the scriptures; for in them ye think ye have eternal life: and they are they which testify of me."

Second, you ought to store up the word of God. In Psalm 119:11, the psalmist said: "Thy word have I hid in mine heart, that I might not sin against thee." That means you ought to commit to memory many portions of the word of God, storing those verses in your heart.

We have all heard about people who were deprived of the word of God for a period of time. In Vietnam some of our prisoners of war were deprived of a copy of the Bible. These men would get together and recall from memory verses in the Bible they had learned in previous years. They put those verses together in order to have Bible study and prayer together. If you were in a similar situation, how much of the word of God would you have in your heart?

Third, you ought to share the word of God with others. In Philippians 2:16 the Bible presents the Christian as "holding forth the word of life." To stay in fellowship with Jesus is to share the word of God.

C. The Spirit of God

Third, to abide in Jesus is also to abide in the Spirit of God. We know that the Spirit abides in us, but the Bible teaches that we ought in turn to abide in the Holy Spirit. Scripture says, "Walk in the Spirit, and ye shall not fulfill the lust of the flesh" (Galatians 5:16). Day by day you ought to yield your life to the indwelling Holy Spirit. As a Christian you have within your life all the power necessary to live a victorious Christian life. Isn't it a shame that we have a dynamite gospel, and we live lives that lack the spark of fireworks? A daily filling of the Spirit will control, cleanse, and change your life!

II. APPEAR

The second word in this sequence is the word *appear*. "Little children, abide in him; that, when he shall appear. . . ." This word introduces us to the theme of the coming again of Jesus. Many beautiful words describe the coming of our Lord. Sometimes, as later in this verse, it is called "his coming." The word means "come alongside" or "be present with." It has to do with an advent or arrival.

"When he shall appear"—here is a prediction that one day the invisible Christ is going to become visible. Hebrews 9:24–28 refers to the three appearings of Jesus, which are taught in the word of God.

Hebrews 9:26 says, "For then must he often have suffered since the foundation of the world: but now once in the end of the world hath he appeared to put away sin by the sacrifice of himself." That verse refers to the first appearing of Jesus. Jesus came into this world two thousand years ago. He appeared to put away sin by the sacrifice of himself.

Another appearing of Jesus Christ is taking place at this moment. "For Christ is not entered into the holy places made with hands, which are the figures of the true; but into heaven itself, now to appear in the presence of God for us" (Hebrews 9:24). That is the present appearing of our Lord. Right now Jesus is in heaven and he appears in heaven for you. Did you know Jesus is praying for you? That ought to be an encouragement to live for him; that ought to encourage us in our daily walk for the Lord.

Another appearing is mentioned in Hebrews 9:28: "So Christ was once offered to bear the sins of many; and unto them that look for him shall he appear the second time without sin unto salvation." This is what we refer to as the second coming, an appearing of Jesus in the future. John says, "When he shall appear, we may have confidence, and not be ashamed before him at his coming."

Certain attitudes ought to be true of all believers in relation to the appearing of our Savior.

A. Looking

We are to be looking for his appearing (Hebrews 9:28). The word means to be patiently waiting, to be looking with anticipation, to be on tiptoe with expectancy for the return of our wonderful Lord. Are you looking for the Lord in that manner? When you study the New Testament you will discover that those early Christians lived in a day-by-day, moment-by-moment expectancy of the return of Jesus Christ. They believed that Jesus could return in their lifetime. They believed that the Lord could come at any moment.

I had a dear step-grandmother whose faith was refreshingly simple. When I was a little boy I used to hear "Aunt Callie" say something like this: "I am looking for Jesus to come back today, but if he does not come back today I am looking for him to come tomorrow." That kind of expectancy should be our attitude.

Some time ago President Ford came to Anderson, South Carolina, only the second time a president of the United States had ever come to the little town of Anderson. I read the newspaper article and I sensed the attitude of the residents as they looked forward to his coming. There was anticipation, expectancy, in that little city because the president of the United States was coming. People were abuzz with activity. They were busy getting things cleaned up and prepared for his arrival. If you are looking for the coming of the Lord Jesus Christ, there will be a sense of urgency in your soul that will vitalize everything you do for God. It will put enthusiasm and fire in your service for him.

B. Loving

We are to be loving his appearing. Second Timothy 4:8 says, "Henceforth there is laid up for me a crown of righteousness, which the Lord, the righteous judge, shall give me at that day: and not to me only, but unto all them also that love his appearing."

First, do you love Jesus? Then, do you love his appearing? There is quite a difference between loving Jesus and loving his appearing.

I have a weakness for chocolate. I don't care what it is, if it is chocolate, I will eat it. If they made chocolate scrambled eggs, I would eat them every time they were served. One day when I was little my mama baked a chocolate cake and gave me strict orders not to touch it. That was just fuel on the fire. Temptation got the best of me. I decided she wouldn't mind if I had just one piece of that chocolate cake, so I cut just one little piece, and it was so good. Then I said, "Well, one calls for another," and so I ate that piece, and before I knew it I cut off another chunk and before I finished I had eaten that whole chocolate cake. I had it all over my face and hands. About that time my mama came driving up in the yard. Now, I loved my mama, but I did not love her appearing!

If we are not careful, we Christians will get wrapped up in this world's pleasures, in this world's possessions, in this world's popularity, and though we love him, we will not love his appearing.

C. Living

We should live looking for the return of our glorious Lord. Titus 2:12–13 says, "Teaching us that, denying ungodliness and worldly lusts, we should live soberly, righteously, and godly, in this present world; Looking for that blessed hope, and the glorious appearing of the great God and our Savior, Jesus Christ." Do you follow the sequence? We are to live every day of our life as though we expect Jesus to come that day.

Bank examiners come by unannounced to check on banks. They may come on Monday, Thursday, Wednesday. They come unexpectedly. Therefore, the folks who work in the banks have to stay on their toes and always be in an attitude of readiness because the examiner might come at any time. We ought to be living daily looking for his appearing.

III. Ashamed

I pray God will search your heart at this point, for I want to deal with this word *ashamed*. "That, when he shall appear, we may have confidence, and not be ashamed before him at his coming." At least three truths are suggested by the word *ashamed*.

A. Appear

First of all, this word suggests that all believers shall appear before Jesus Christ. Some Christians have the idea that when they are saved it does not really matter how they live. They think they are going to get to heaven regardless. They think God will skip over some of the things they have done. They think the things they have done as a Christian will never be brought up before them again.

It is a truth that our sins have been put away forever under the blood of the Lord Jesus Christ. It is also a truth that you and I as Christians will appear before the judgment seat of Christ to give an account for the kind of life we have lived since we received him as our Savior. Second Corinthians 5:10 says, "For we [Christians] must all appear before the judgment seat of Christ; that every one may receive the things done in his body according to that he hath done, whether it be good or bad."

Romans 14:10–12 says that we must all stand before the judgment seat of Christ, and that every one of us must give an account to God. First Corinthians 3 says that a day is going to come when the believer's works will be tried by fire. Works that are not lasting, not Christ-exalting and Christ-honoring, will go up in smoke. Only what has been done for Jesus Christ will remain.

B. Acceptable

Some believers are going to be acceptable before him. I did not say accepted; I said acceptable. Every Christian is accepted. Ephesians 1:6 says we are "accepted in the beloved." The only way you can ever possibly go to heaven is to be accepted in Jesus Christ. A righteousness not your own is bestowed on you, imputed to you by the Lord Jesus Christ, and you are accepted in Christ, accepted in the beloved. If you are saved, you are accepted.

However, there is a lot of difference between being accepted and being acceptable. Let me use another simple illustration. Here is a little fellow whose mother gets him all dressed up for Sunday school. She has his hair combed just right, and his face scrubbed, and she has his little coat on him and his little shoes shined. She says, "You can go out on the porch, but I want you to stay clean." You know what that little fellow does. He sees other children down the street and he decides to go down the street. He fails to notice that there is mud on the road. It has been raining. About Sunday school time he gets back to the house and he is muddy from top to bottom. His mother will accept him, but he certainly is not acceptable.

If you are truly born again, you are accepted, but when you stand before Jesus Christ, you may not be acceptable. The kind of life you live, the kind of habits you have, and the kind of testimony you have borne for the Lord Jesus Christ will determine your acceptability. If we abide in him, we will be able to have confidence at his coming. The word *confidence* means openness, freedom of speech, no sense of restraint; it means to be so close to Jesus and so in fellowship with him that we will not freeze in his presence.

C. Ashamed

Some Christians are going to be ashamed before him. The original scripture here is much more picturesque than the King James version. It really means "may be ashamed from him." It could be translated "shall shrink in shame from him." When Jesus comes, some Christians will be so embarrassed, their life will be so inconsistent, that when they see him, they will shrink in shame.

Jesus is going to catch some Christians redhanded with things in their life they do not want there when Jesus comes. Wouldn't it be terrible for Jesus to come and catch a Christian writing poison pen letters? Wouldn't it be awful for Jesus to come and find you displaying your old nature? Isn't it going to be a shame for Jesus to come and find some Christians who are not speaking to other Christians? Isn't it tragic for Christians to allow malice and envy to infect their heart? Won't it be embarrassing for the Lord to come and find some Christian with a big black cigar in his hand? All the way up in the rapture he will be trying to get rid of that cigar, and he will stand at the judgment seat still trying to hide it.

When Dwight Eisenhower was president he vacationed in Denver, Colorado. There was in Denver a six-year-old boy who had incurable cancer. The boy expressed the wish that he might see President Eisenhower. One Sunday morning President Eisenhower arrived in his presidential limousine. He walked up to the front door and knocked. The father opened the door in his blue jeans and old shirt and with a day's growth of beard. When he saw the president, he was speechless! The president took the six-year-old boy out to see the limousine and talked with him for a while. Then he shook his hand and left. For many days after that the father would recount the story and say, "And just to think, there I stood with my blue jeans, my old shirt, and a day's growth of beard. What a way to meet the president!" Wouldn't it be embarrassing for our Lord to appear and for us to have to shrink in shame before him? Little children, abide in him, so that when he appears, you will not shrink in shame at his coming.

9

It's Out of This World
1 John 3:1–3

   I. OUR POSITION
     A. Selected by the Father
     B. Slighted by the World
  II. OUR POTENTIAL
     A. Anticipated
     B. Actualized
 III. OUR PRACTICE
     A. Hopefulness
     B. Holiness

As HAS BEEN SAID, THE FIRST TWO CHAPTERS OF JOHN'S EPISTLE HAVE AS their main theme the subject of fellowship. The key verse is verse 5 of chapter 1: "God is light." Fellowship with God is on the basis of our walking in the light as he is in the light.

The next three chapters have the subject of sonship as their theme. The key verse is 4:8: "God is love." You and I are children of God, we are in the family of God, because of the amazing love of God.

D. L. Moody gave himself to a study of love in the Bible. He traced through a Bible concordance all of the references in the word of God to the subject of love. As he studied and got into it more deeply, he discovered he just couldn't help but love people. The love of God seemed to be flowing from his fingertips to other people. As we consider the subject of the love of God I pray that we will come to a new experience of God's love, this love that is truly out of this world.

I want us to learn three lessons about those who are the children of God.

I. OUR POSITION

First, these verses clearly describe our position, what we are: We are the children of God right now. I remember how God brought this particular truth home to my heart. I was journeying one night from a revival meeting and I was turning the dial of my radio from station to station. I picked up a man on the radio who is one of the best-known false teachers of our day. Just about any time of the day you can listen to this man and he will be propounding his particular version of heresy. On this night he was making fun of the concept that it is possible to be born of God and actually to be a son of God right now. He believes that you cannot be a son of God until you get to heaven, and only when you get into heaven will you be born again and become a son of God. He was laughing at this idea and he asked, "Whoever heard of a person being right now the son of God?" In a flash the Holy Spirit brought to my memory 1 John 3:2, "Beloved, now are we the sons of God." If we know Jesus as Savior, we are children of God right now.

A. Selected by the Father

As the children of God we are selected by the Father. First John 3:1 teaches that we are children of God because God has chosen us to be recipients of his love. John is amazed at the love of God that made it possible for him to be in God's family. He says simply, Take a look at it, take a look at this kind of love. "Behold, what manner of love the Father hath bestowed upon us."

I don't think we will ever understand the love of God until we get to heaven. John 3:16 says, "For God so loved the world. . . ." I wonder what is contained in that little word *so*. How much does it mean, how far does it go, when the Bible says that "God so loved the world . . ."?

The word *so* tells us several things about the love of God—first, the love of God is undeserved. John says, ". . . what manner of love the Father hath bestowed upon us," we who are so undeserving. The love of God is like a river that flows out of the heart of God and reaches us wherever we are. It does not matter how low a man may go in sin. It does not matter how far away a person may get from God, the love of God reaches down and meets us in the depths of our need, in the pits of our human experience.

Many years ago a little girl who had been disfigured in a fire was taken to a children's home. Her face was scarred and unbecoming. When along with some other children she was brought to the train terminal where the superintendent of the children's home would pick her up, she stood off in the corner and watched as the superintendent picked up the others, hugged them, and smothered them with kisses. After a while she edged up beside the superintendent and said, "Please, mister, I know I am not pretty like the other little girls; I know that my face doesn't look too good, but would you mind hugging me just a little bit? You don't have to kiss me, but would you just hug me and let me know you're glad I'm here?" Well, of course, you know what he did. He reached down and took that child with the scarred face, wrapped her in his arms, and smothered that scarred face with kisses. So it is with the love of God.

God's love is so unselfish that he gave his only Son. "But God commendeth [exhibits] his love toward us, in that, while we were yet sinners, Christ died for us" (Romans 5:8). The Son of God became the Son of man in order to make it possible for the sons of men to become the sons of God.

Also, this verse teaches us that the love of God is unique. John says, "Look at what manner of love, what quality love," or it could be translated "from what country," is this kind of love. It is interesting to notice the other places where this particular word occurs. We find it in Mark 4:39–41. Jesus calmed the storm. He had said to the waves, "Peace, be still." The waves were still and the men who saw it proclaimed, "What manner of man is this, that even the wind and the sea obey him?" From what country is this man? What kind of man, what otherworldly man is this, who has this kind of power?

The word is found again in 2 Peter 3:11, where it talks about the second coming of the Lord and the dissolving of this world in the last days: "What manner of persons ought ye to be?" The love that God bestows on us, making us his children, is a love altogether otherworldly, unearthly. It is an out-of-this-world kind of love.

When Balboa discovered the Pacific Ocean, he was so thrilled that he fell on his knees weeping and thanked God for the honor of such a discovery. This is what John must have felt when he said, "Behold, what manner of love. . . ." When it dawned on his soul how wonderful the love of God is, all he could do was celebrate it and rejoice in it and experience it. He did not try to define it, he did not try to explain it; all he could do was thank God for it.

B. Slighted by the World

The first verse of 1 John 3 has a second truth: We are slighted by the world: "Therefore the world knoweth us not, because it knew him not." The world did not know Jesus. That is a paradox. John 1:10–11 says, "He was in the world, and the world was made by him, and the world knew him not. He came unto his own, and his own received him not."

The world did not recognize Jesus. They did not know who he was. They should have recognized him; they should have known that Jesus Christ was no mere man. No mere man ever before had lived as Jesus lived on this earth. No mere man had done the things Jesus did. No ordinary man could have lived that kind of life, yet this world did not recognize him. The old spiritual puts it well: "Sweet little Jesus boy, we didn't know who you was." So they mistreated the Son of God. They did wrong to this heavenly visitor who came into the world for one purpose, to die for the sins of the world.

Because the world did not know Jesus, John says, "The world will not know you either." The world will not recognize you. The world will not appreciate who you are and to whom you belong. You see, this world has no idea of what it has in its midst. In fact, I have just about decided that the world does not know anything worth knowing. The world knows how to make us unhappy. The world knows how to build bigger and better buildings. But it does not know the things that really matter. In the midst of this world there is a group of people. They are strange to some, unusual to others, and they are the objects of this world's ridicule and scorn, yet God says they are the children of the king. They are the children of the God of this universe, and the world knows them not. They are passing through this world as pilgrims and strangers. They do not belong down here.

The little town I came from in Georgia had as one of its citizens for a few years the actress Susan Hayward, who won an academy award for her performance in *I Want to Live*. Upon her return to Carrollton they had a big celebration. Signs welcomed their favorite, most famous citizen back to the little city. I had been away from Carrollton for some years and was making a visit back home that particular day. When I got to town I looked up and saw signs welcoming Susan. I saw signs saying, "We want you to live here, Susan." I came riding in just a little while before Susan and nobody knew I was coming. No one seemed to be thrilled about it. You see, the world is not interested in the children of God.

This world is interested in fame and beauty. This world is interested in skill, attainment, and worldly achievement. It has very little interest in the things of God. And so as the children of God we are slighted by this world. We ought not to be surprised when we are not in this world's Hall of Fame. We ought not to be disturbed when we are not recognized, honored, and given fame by this world.

II. Our Potential

"Beloved, now are we the sons of God [that is what we are now], and it doth not yet appear what we shall be." That is our potential. That is what we shall be. If you are a Christian, you are not what you used to be, thank God. You may not be what you ought to be, but you are not what you are going to be by the grace of God. Great potential lies ahead for all of God's children.

A. Anticipated

In this passage of scripture we see our potential anticipated. John says, "It doth not yet appear what we shall be." I can almost feel the anticipation in his words. I can almost sense John's excitement as he says, "Why, we have not seen yet what God has in store for those who really belong to him." God has a thrilling destiny for his children. There is going to be a wonderful appearance; there is going to be a wonderful time of display when God is going to show off his children, show the world what they really are. Colossians 3:4 says, "When Christ, who is our life, shall appear, then shall ye also appear with him in glory." A great day awaits the people of God.

The promise that there is more to come distinguishes the destiny of the lost person and the saved person. If you are lost, the most wretched experience that can come to your life is to grow old. Think about growing old without Jesus Christ. There is only one way for you to look, and that is back, and much of that is unpleasant. Wouldn't it be a tragedy to come to the end of your life without Christ, never knowing him as your Savior, looking back on a lifetime of regret and wasted existence? You dare not look to the future. The most miserable people on the face of God's green earth are those who are lost and are going on in their sin. They have nothing to anticipate.

But the best thing that can happen to you in this life is to grow old in anticipation of what God has for you. Some of the happiest Christians I have met are people who have a little gray on their heads. Some of the liveliest, most enthusiastic, wide-awake Christians are among those we would normally call senior citizens. They are just beginning to live. They are just getting warmed up for the big show out there in the future.

B. Actualized

"When he shall appear. . . ." When Jesus comes, everything God intended when he saved you is going to be actualized. God saved you in order to make you like Jesus. You may not be much like him now. I am not much like him either. We may not resemble Jesus much now but if we are saved, one of these days when he appears we are going to be like the Son of God.

Notice what John says about the actualization of our potential. When Jesus appears at least two things will take place: One, he says we shall see him as he is. Think of it. We are actually going to see the Lord Jesus Christ. You have never seen Jesus with the eyes of your physical body, have you? Neither have I.

We have no pictures of our Lord. We do not know how he really looks.

Men have gone off to war and while they were gone babies have been born into their home. They have never seen them. The wives have sent pictures to the father, and through pictures they have gotten some idea of what their baby looks like, but how they long for the day when they will not look at pictures anymore but will see that daughter or son face to face.

We have never seen Jesus, but God has given us pictures of him in the four gospels. We can get a glimpse of him, but some day our faith will turn to sight. The Bible says, "Whom having not seen, ye love; in whom, though now ye see him not, yet believing, ye rejoice with joy unspeakable and full of glory" (1 Peter 1:8). Although we have not seen him, we love him.

We have a picture of that in Genesis 24, the story of the servant of Abraham seeking a bride for Isaac. When he found Rebecca, he told her about his master. All he could do was tell her. There were no pictures to show. Although she had never seen Isaac, the moment of decision came. The father looked at Rebecca and looked at the servant. Then he looked back at Rebecca and asked, "Are you willing to go?" She made her decision. She said, "I will go!"

It must have been quite a journey. She was riding on a camel, and camels go only about three miles per hour. It must have become quite wearying through those hot, dusty roads, looking forward to seeing this man she had never seen before. That is the way it is with a Christian. Sometimes the road gets dusty. Sometimes we wonder, "Will I ever make it, will I ever get there?"

Then one day along about sunset, Isaac was out meditating in the field. The caravan came in sight of Isaac, and the servant saw his master. He said to Rebecca, "My master!" The Bible says when she saw him she got off the camel and went to meet her future husband. Faith had become sight. One glorious day our Lord will appear and when he does, the "camels" of this earth will lose their importance and we will be enraptured with a face-to-face meeting.

The Bible says also that we shall be like him—like Jesus. We are going to be conformed to the image of God's dear Son. What will it mean to be like Jesus? I think it means at least three things.

First, it will mean purity of character. Our character will be as pure as the Lord Jesus Christ. We have problems with that down here. We have trouble with sin down here. One of these days our character will be purified. We will be saved, to sin no more.

Second, it will mean glorification in body. Philippians 3:21 says that he will change these vile bodies, these bodies of humiliation, that they might be fashioned like his glorious body. You are going to have a new body when you see Jesus. Your body is going to be perfect and it going to be glorified like the body of the Son of God.

Blind people will see him when Jesus comes again. Lame people will walk. Deaf people will hear. Those who are mute will talk. There will be no deficiency, no disease, no death, in these bodies of ours when we see Jesus.

Third, there will be satisfaction of heart. Psalm 17:15 says, "As for me, I will behold thy face in righteousness: I shall be satisfied, when I awake, with thy likeness." We will be completely satisfied. Our soul will never again thirst for things eternal. We will see him and be like him. That is our potential.

III. OUR PRACTICE

"And every man that hath this hope in him purifieth himself, even as he is pure" (1 John 3:3). In our daily practice as children of God we ought to be both hopeful and holy.

A. Hopefulness

Where is your hope? On what does your hope rest? John's words, "Every man that hath this hope in him," actually ought to be translated "Every man that has his hope set on him." The emphasis is not on the hope in your heart, but on that on which your hope is resting.

This world puts its hope in banks, savings institutions, military power, leaders. That is why when people lose those things, they are like someone going through a desert who comes to a mirage and instead of finding what will quench his thirst, he finds only parching sand. If your hope is on anything but Jesus it is wasted.

> My hope is built on nothing less
> Than Jesus' blood and righteousness.

B. Holiness

John says that those who have their hope set on him purify themselves even as he is pure. The second coming of Jesus rightly understood is an incentive to live a daily life of holiness. If we are expecting Jesus to appear, if we really believe that the Son of God could come at any moment, it will have a tremendous constraining effect on our daily life; it will cause us to want to live like Jesus.

It says here, "He is pure." Two words are translated as "pure" in the New Testament. One is the word *purity*, in the sense in which God is absolutely pure. Another word, the one used here, means a purity maintained in the face of temptation, a purity sustained through terrific trial and strain. When it says that Jesus is pure, it means Jesus possessed a purity that he maintained through the temptations, stresses, and problems he encountered. What if Jesus had only once let impurity get into his life? He would have at that moment been disqualified to be our Savior. My Savior and your Savior loved us so much that he maintained his purity.

Likewise, our love for Jesus ought to cause us to maintain our purity for him. If we really love him, we will want to live in a way that will not disappoint him. A young girl was out with friends one night, far from home, and her friends suggested that they go to a questionable place. She hesitated for a moment and then said, "I think I had better not go."

One of her friends said sarcastically, "Are you afraid if you go your father might hurt you?"

The girl replied, "No, I am not afraid my father might hurt me if I go, but I am afraid if I go, I might hurt my father." That ought to be the attitude in our heart. We ought to want to maintain our purity of life lest we hurt him, lest we bring reproach on his name.

A pure life is a daily process.

Certainly there is a sense in which God purifies us. Titus 2:14 says that he is purifying unto himself a peculiar people, zealous of good works. It is kind of like soap. Soap will make you pure, but you have to use it. God has given you his word, prayer, and the means of grace by which you can keep your life clean and pure every day. They are given by him, but you must use them.

A soldier went through all the battles of the European campaign. Amid the revelry, all that went on, this man kept himself above reproach. The others noticed that he would not participate in some of the things they were doing. Finally they asked him about it. Bill answered, "Back home there is a girl I love with all my heart. When this war is over, I am going to be married to that girl and I am keeping myself just for her."

Just over the clouds there is a Savior who loved us and gave himself for us. We ought to want to keep ourselves pure and clean for him. One day, when he comes, we are going to be married to him.

10

Sinless Perfection
1 John 3:4–10

I. THE PROVISION OF THE SAVIOR
   A. The Necessity of His Provision
   B. The Nature of His Provision
II. THE PRACTICE OF THE SAINTS
   A. They Do Not Practice Sin
   B. They Do Practice Righteousness
III. THE POWER OF SALVATION
   A. A New Dynamic
   B. A New Desire
   C. A New Deterrent

OUR TEXT NOW BRINGS US FACE TO FACE WITH ONE OF THE MOST DIFFIcult and crucial questions in the Bible. Does the Bible teach that it is possible for a Christian to live above sin? It is obvious as we read these verses of scripture that on the surface they seem to teach that a person who is a child of God does not sin. Many honest and sincere groups of Christian people have taken these verses and other verses in the Bible and from them have taught that it is possible for a person who is born again to live above sin in daily life. To take that view, to teach the doctrine of sinless perfection, results in insurmountable difficulties.

First, to teach the doctrine of sinless perfection is contradictory to what we know in human experience. When we read about the great men in the Bible, we discover that though they were true believers in the Lord, they sometimes sinned. The apostle Paul says, "Not as though I had already attained, either were already perfect . . ." (Philippians 3:12). Paul made clear that he did not live above sin. Also, when we observe closely the lives of those who say that they live above sin, we come to see that what they profess with their lips is not consistent with what they practice with their life.

Further, when we look into our own heart and at our life, we find the disturbing fact that the possibility and potentiality of sin are there even though we have received Jesus as Savior. Because some groups have the idea that if they are saved they are going to have to live above sin, many immature Christians get discouraged in their Christian life and fall by the wayside when sin overtakes them. They receive Jesus as their Savior, they are baptized, they begin to live for the Lord, and they do well until they sin. Then it is a shattering experience in their life and, believing that a Christian will not sin, they come to the conclusion that they were never saved in the first place—or that they were saved and have lost their salvation. When you talk to people in those circumstances and ask, "Are you a Christian?" they will say, "Well, I used to be. I am not now, but I used to be." What they mean is that they have let sin get into their life and because they believe the Bible teaches sinless perfection, they do not believe that they are any longer a child of God.

This raises a serious objection to the doctrine of sinless perfection. It is a flagrant contradiction to what is taught in 1 John 1:8–10. "If we say that we have no sin, we deceive ourselves, and the truth is not in us. If we say that we have not sinned, we make him a liar, and his word is not in us."

The Bible does not contradict itself. The Bible is consistent throughout. We must conclude on the basis of those simple statements of the word of God that the doctrine of sinless perfection is not taught in the Bible.

It is not possible for a child of God to live above sin in this world. Having come to that conclusion, how then are we to interpret these verses of scripture? What does the Bible mean when it says, "Whosoever is born of God doth not commit sin . . . and he cannot sin, because he is born of God" (1 John 3:9)? We must be careful to adhere to the admonition of Paul to rightly divide the word of truth.

I. The Provision of the Savior

First, we have the provision of the Savior. When the Lord Jesus Christ came into the world and died on the cross of Calvary he made perfect provision for daily victory over the problem of sin in the life of the child of God.

A. The Necessity of His Provision

"Whosoever committeth sin transgresseth also the law: for sin is the transgression of the law" (1 John 3:4). Why did Jesus come into this world? What is the meaning of his leaving the ivory palaces of heaven and coming down into a world such as ours to go through what he went through, to endure what he endured, to be crucified? This verse of scripture makes it obvious that human sinfulness made the cross necessary. Sin is to blame. If man had not sinned, then Jesus Christ need not have come. But because sin entered into the human family it was imperative that the Son of God should come into this world.

Here we are given a simple definition of sin, one of many definitions of sin in the Bible. Because sin is a many-headed monster, it is impossible for one term to define adequately what sin is and what sin does. James 4:17 says, "Therefore to him that knoweth to do good, and doeth it not, to him it is sin." Romans 14:23 says, "For whatsoever is not of faith is sin." In 1 John 5:17 we read, "All unrighteousness is sin." But 1 John 3:4 gives a simple, concise definition of sin: "Sin is the transgression of the law." The word sin means to step over the boundary line, to violate the commandments of God. God said to Adam and Eve in the garden of Eden, "You can eat fruit from all the trees in this garden except one, but you are not to eat fruit from that tree. When you do, you will surely die." Adam and Eve disobeyed God. They stepped over the line that God had drawn and when they did, sin came into their life.

Sin is rebellion against God. Sin is spiritual anarchy. Scripture teaches, "For all have sinned, and come short of the glory of God" (Romans 3:23). When people sin they are saying to God, "God, I don't care what you say about it. I don't care what you want. I want to have it my way. I am going to do it my way." Now it is all right to "have it your way" if you want mustard or pickles on your hamburger, but it is not right to have it your way when it contradicts what God has said in the Bible.

B. The Nature of His Provision

I want to consider also the nature of our Lord's work. We are told both in 1 John 3:5 and 8 why the Son of God was manifested. Let us look at two of the reasons why Jesus Christ made the provision of Calvary.

In 1 Timothy 1:15 the Bible says, "This is a faithful saying, and worthy of all acceptation, that Christ Jesus came into the world to save sinners; of whom I am chief." In Luke 19:10 Jesus said, "For the Son of man is come to seek and to save that which was lost." But 1 John gives us further understanding.

The first purpose of Jesus' coming was to deal with sin. "And ye know that he was manifested to take away our sins; and in him is no sin" (1 John 3:5). Jesus came to take away sin. If I brought a message every Sunday about the cross of Jesus Christ, in a millennium of sermons I would not exhaust all of the glories of the cross. Among the many things Jesus did at the cross, he completely dealt with the sin question. In John 1:29 John the baptist saw Jesus coming and said, "Behold the Lamb of God, which taketh away the sin of the world." Hebrews 9:26 says, "Now once in the end of the world hath he appeared to put away sin by the sacrifice of himself." Jesus dealt with the old sin nature, the rebellion in the human heart. Jesus dealt with the guilt and penalty of sin when he died on the cross of Calvary.

He died not only for sin, but for your sin. If you got out a sheet of paper and began to list all of the sins you have committed in your life, you would fill up the front of the page and then the back of the page. You could try to write all of your sins, but you would never get through. So, my brothers and sisters, let us rejoice in the fact that when Jesus Christ went to the cross, he put those sins away and buried them forever. First Peter 2:24 teaches that Christ bore our sins in his own body on the tree. In the book of Leviticus there is a picture of this twofold truth about how Jesus dealt with sin totally.

In Leviticus 16 we are told that two lambs would be brought to the high priest. The first lamb was for the sin offering. The second lamb was known as the scapegoat, and over that animal were confessed the sins of the people. Then they would take the scapegoat out into a wilderness place to send it away forever. Isn't it wonderful to know that Jesus was manifested to take away our sins, to lift them up off us, and to carry them away?

Jesus has made provision for you. There is no need for you to sin; Jesus has dealt with your sins. He has removed your sins and, when you sin, you do it in spite of the provision he has made.

The second purpose of Jesus' coming was to deal with Satan. "For this purpose the Son of God was manifested, that he might destroy the works of the devil" (1 John 3:8). It is the devil's job to tempt you to sin. When Jesus died, he did something that put the devil out of commission.

In these verses we see the provision of the Savior. We do not have to sin. Sometimes those who do not believe in sinless perfection are accused of teaching a sinning religion. They say, "Baptist folk believe that they can sin a little every day." I do not believe that. I do not think we have to sin a little every day. The Lord Jesus Christ has made it possible for us to have victory over daily sins in our life. We do not have to be defeated by the devil. We do not have to be defeated by sin. We can live a life of victory.

II. The Practice of the Saints

Here John makes two clear statements about the children of God. His first assertion is found in 1 John 3:6. "Whosoever abideth in him sinneth not: whosoever sinneth hath not seen him, neither known him."

A. They Do Not Practice Sin

The child of God does not practice sin. I did not say the child of God does not commit an act of sin. Certainly there are times in the life of a Christian when we do something we ought not to do; we commit an act of sin. But the Bible teaches that the child of God does not practice sin.

At this point the tenses of the Greek verbs are important. The King James version of the Bible was translated in 1611 and has been used by the English-speaking world since that time with great effectiveness. We can understand the language of the King James version and be blessed by it.

In 1611, however, a clear distinction was not made in the verb tenses used here, and they are crucial in interpreting this passage of scripture. When the Bible says, "Whosoever abideth in him sinneth not," the verb is present tense. In the New American Standard Bible, it is put this way, "Whosoever is born of God does not practice sin." The Living Bible paraphrases it, "If you are born of God you do not keep on sinning." The New International Version emphatically states: "No one who lives in him, keeps on sinning. No one who continues to sin has either seen him or known him."

John is not saying that you may not commit an isolated act of sin. He is saying that if you are born of God, it is not the habit of your life to go on and on sinning. You may occasionally sin if you are a child of God, but you will habitually want to do what is right. The pattern of your life is not to sin; the practice of your life is not to sin. Those who are saved do not keep on sinning.

Conversely, if you do go on sinning, if you do practice sinning, then you are not of God, and you do not know him. Verse 10 of 1 John 3 says you are of the devil if you go on and on sinning. The man, woman, or young person who constantly and habitually sins is not born of God. If you are saved, you do not make it a practice to sin.

Let me illustrate in this manner. Here is a professional football player. He is an all-pro, and a master at this position. He knows how to carry out his assignments. He knows what his responsibilities are, and so he normally and habitually performs his task as he ought to perform it. He normally carries out his assignments, but occasionally he may miss an assignment. He may miss a block, but that is the exception and not the rule in his performance. It is the same with the Christian life. Sin in the life of a Christian is the exception and not the rule. If you are born of God you do not practice sin.

B. They Do Practice Righteousness

A second truth is this: if you are a child of God you practice righteousness. "Little children, let no man deceive you: he that doeth righteousness [that is, the person who habitually does right, who makes it a practice to do right things] is righteous, even as he is righteous" (1 John 3:7). Lost people do good occasionally, of course.

Do I believe in the total depravity of man? Of course I do. The Bible teaches it. Why is it then that sometimes those who are lost, who are not Christians, will be philanthropic with their money and will do a lot of wonderful things? My reply is that the lost occasionally may do right, but habitually do wrong.

In Matthew 7:17 Jesus says that a corrupt tree brings forth corrupt fruit and a good tree brings forth good fruit. Occasionally you might get a good apple off a bad tree and occasionally you might get a bad apple off a good tree, but normally the fruits of a good tree will be good. So it is in the life of the child of God. That is what John is saying here. He is not saying that you will never sin if you are a child of God. Rather, he is saying that the trend of your life is toward God. The main direction of your life is toward doing those things that please him.

III. The Power of Salvation

The power of salvation is tremendous when it comes into a human life.

A. A New Dynamic

First John 3:9 begins and ends with the phrase "born of God." John is talking about the experience of being born again. When you become a child of God, an altogether new dimension is added to your life; a new dynamic comes into your life. When we are born of God, his seed, a new nature, remains in us. The new life we receive from God at the moment of salvation is the seed, the new dynamic.

If you are lost, you have only one nature. If you are unsaved, you have only one nature, which you received at the moment of birth. You have an old nature, an Adam nature, and you have no ultimate choice except to yield to that nature because it is the only nature you have. You may resist temptation for a while, but if you are lost, sooner or later temptation is going to conquer you because you have an unregenerate nature. You have the old nature, and you are completely under its control.

If you are a child of God, you have a new nature. A new dynamic is inside you. When temptation, the opportunity to sin comes, you now have the choice either to be dominated by your old nature or to be dominated by the new nature. If you are dominated by the old nature, you are a carnal Christian. If you are dominated by the new nature, you are a spiritual Christian. That is what salvation does for you.

B. A New Desire

Second, there is an altogether new desire when Jesus comes into your life. You not only do not want to sin, but you want to do what is right. Romans 7:22 says, "I delight in the law of God after the inward man." When salvation comes, you want to do God's law. You do not want to be a rebel anymore. You do not want to be a spiritual anarchist anymore. Hebrews 8:10 says that God writes his law in your heart, and then the desire of your life is to serve Jesus and to do right. Sometimes you fail the Lord, you are not all you ought to be, but down in your heart you can truthfully say, "Jesus, I want to do what you want me to do."

An old Methodist evangelist named Dr. Morrison taught the doctrine of holiness, and it was said that he came closer to practicing it than most folks do. Someone said to Dr. Morrison jokingly, "Dr. Morrison have you gotten to where you cannot sin?" Dr. Morrison said, "No, my brother, I have not yet gotten to where I cannot sin, but I have gotten to where I cannot sin and enjoy it." That is where I am. I cannot sin and enjoy it. Can you?

Do you know what changed my opinion about sin and put me out of the sin-enjoying business? It was realizing that every time I sinned, another sin was laid on the Lord Jesus Christ at the cross of Calvary and was added to the load he bore there. It broke my heart. I have never since been able to enjoy doing things I ought not to do because I know that those are the very things that caused Jesus to groan in agony on the cross. You cannot enjoy sin for long if you are a child of God.

C. A New Deterrent

When Jesus comes into your life, there is also a new deterrent down in your heart: "His seed remaineth in him: and he cannot sin, because he is born of God." That means we cannot practice sin. Not only will we not practice sin, but we cannot practice sin.

Ephesians 4:30 says, "And grieve not the holy Spirit of God, whereby ye are sealed unto the day of redemption." When we sin, it grieves the Holy Spirit. When sin gets in our life as a Christian, it becomes a challenge to the Holy Spirit. It becomes another lover in our heart and the Holy Spirit of God will not share his dwelling place with any sin. Our new nature starts fighting that sin, the Holy Spirit of God starts grieving our soul, and we are smitten in conscience. We lose our fellowship with God, our peace, our joy. We lose the love that comes through knowing and serving the Lord and being in fellowship with him. Sin grieves us until we confess it and God cleanses it. We cannot just keep on sinning, if we are really saved.

How do we get victory over sin? In 1 Corinthians 15:45 the Bible talks about the old Adam (the first Adam, it is called there), our old nature. "The last Adam" is Jesus. When temptation comes knocking at the door of our heart, we have one of two choices. We can send the old Adam to the door; and when we do, we will sin. But when temptation comes knocking at the door, we can send the last Adam to the door. When Jesus goes to the door, we get victory over that sin. That is how we do it. Every day let Jesus take over. Let Jesus answer the door when temptation knocks.

Are you a child of God? Are you born again? "But as many as received him, to them gave he power to become the sons of God." I want you to become a child of God. I want you to receive this new nature that will give you the potential of victory over sin every day of your life.

11

Satan Is Alive but Not Well
1 John 3:8

I. THE ORIGIN OF THE DEVIL
   A. A Created Being
   B. A Corrupted Being
   C. A Condemned Being
II. THE OPERATION OF THE DEVIL
   A. Mentally
   B. Morally
   C. Motivationally
III. THE OVERTHROW OF THE DEVIL
   A. Commenced by Jesus
   B. Continued by the Saints
   C. Consummated at the Final Judgment

IN RECENT YEARS MAGAZINES, MOVIES, AND MUSIC HAVE HAD A RENEWED EMphasis on the subject of the devil and the powerful forces of evil in our world. Even the secular press has noted a revival of interest in witchcraft, the occult, and even Satan worship.

Such publicity has caused Bible-believing scholars to go again to the word of God and investigate its teachings on the subject. The result of their investigation has been an explosion of books and pamphlets on the devil and demonology in the world today. Some of the books have been very good and sound; others have been more sensational than helpful.

It seems to me that there is almost an unhealthy obsession today with the subject of the devil. It is important to acquaint yourself with any subject in the word of God, but there is a danger in spending more time thinking and talking about the devil than about Jesus. Christians ought to rivet their mind and heart on the Lord, that every thought be brought into captivity to the obedience of Christ (2 Corinthians 10:5). The Bible says, "Thou wilt keep him in perfect peace, whose mind is stayed on thee: because he trusteth in thee" (Isaiah 26:3). This chapter therefore is not intended to give undue emphasis to the subject of the devil, but to deal with it as it is dealt with in the word of God. My purpose is to show from the word of God how the power of the devil is antedated, anticipated, and annulled by the power of the Lord Jesus Christ.

I. The Origin of the Devil

"He that committeth sin is of the devil; for the devil sinneth from the beginning" (1 John 3:8). Who is the devil? Where does the devil come from? What does the Bible have to say about him? Nowhere in the word of God is there an attempt to prove the identity of the devil. It is everywhere assumed that an actual personality known as the devil exists. In Ezekiel 28, we see three main lines of truth taught about the origin of the devil. First I want you to see that the devil is a created being, second that he is a corrupted being, and third that he is a condemned being.

A. A Created Being

Ezekiel 28:11ff is an unusual passage of scripture. The primary reference is to the king of Tyrus. But as we read we cannot avoid the conclusion that a more sinister personality than the king of Tyrus is intended by these verses. I believe we have here insight into the origin of the devil, who he is and where he came from. "Son of man, take up a lamentation upon the king of Tyrus, and say unto him, Thus saith the Lord God; Thou sealest

up the sum, full of wisdom, and perfect in beauty. Thou hast
been in Eden the garden of God; every precious stone was thy
covering, the sardius, topaz, and the diamond, the beryl, the
onyx, and the jasper, the sapphire, the emerald, and the car-
buncle, and gold: the workmanship of thy tabrets and of thy
pipes was prepared in thee in the day that thou wast created"
(Ezekiel 28:12–13). In verse 15 we read these words, "Thou wast
perfect in thy ways from the day that thou wast created." Two
times in this passage we are taught that the devil is a created
being. Verse 14 teaches that he was created as an anointed
cherub.

A cherub in the word of God seems to have been the highest
order of angelic beings in heaven. The devil was the anointed
cherub, created and set apart for a specific purpose. "Thou art
the anointed cherub that covereth." The word *covereth* might
well be translated "that guardeth." This anointed cherub was
set aside for the specific purpose of guarding access to the
throne of God. We notice something else in verse 13. It says of
him, "Thou hast been in Eden the garden of God." When we
read that, we think immediately of Genesis 3. We know that the
devil was in the garden of Eden, tempted Adam and Eve, and
brought sin into the world. However, that allusion is not what is
intended here. This was an Eden constituted as a mineral kingdom. Precious stones are named in this particular Eden of God.
When you look at Genesis 3 you find something altogether different. You find there an Eden that was constituted of plant life.
Trees of all kinds were in that garden.

In verse 13 and following it mentions tabrets and pipes. In
Isaiah 14 viols are mentioned; every major kind of musical instrument is mentioned in relationship to the devil. I personally
see this as an indication that the devil was heaven's music
angel. I believe he was assigned to lead the heavenly choirs in
praise and adoration of God.

B. A Corrupted Being

"Thou wast perfect in thy ways from the day that thou wast
created, till iniquity was found in thee" (Ezekiel 28:15). The
devil became a corrupted being. Verse 17 says, "Thine heart

was lifted up because of thy beauty, thou hast corrupted thy wisdom by reason of thy brightness." These verses indicate that the devil fell and became corrupted for a particular reason. In Isaiah 14:9ff we see that the primary reference is to the prince of Babylon. However, we can see emerging also in these verses a sinister, shadowy figure who I believe is none other than the devil himself. Notice what is said in verse 12. "How art thou fallen from heaven, O Lucifer, son of the morning! how art thou cut down to the ground, which didst weaken the nations!" Notice why the devil fell. "For thou hast said in thine heart [that is, the devil said], I will ascend into heaven, I will exalt my throne above the stars of God: I will sit also upon the mount of the congregation in the sides of the north: I will ascend above the heights of the clouds; I will be like the most High" (Isaiah 14:12–14). The devil was not content merely to guard the throne of God. He also coveted it. He was not content to be a special angel, not content to be a servant of the most high God. Rather, he sought to usurp God's throne. He said in his heart, I will lift myself up above the throne of God.

The word of God teaches that "pride goeth before destruction, and an haughty spirit before a fall" (Proverbs 16:18). How true that is. The moment you allow pride to come into your heart, at that moment God says, "You are headed for a fall."

What is true in your life and my life was true of the devil. The devil said, "I am going up"; God said, "You are going down." The devil fell because of the sin of pride. He was proud of his beauty and brightness, so he sought to revolt against God himself, to thrust God from the throne of the universe. The Bible says that God cast the devil out of heaven. "Yet thou shalt be brought down to hell to the side of the pit" (Isaiah 14:15). Our Savior makes mention of this in Luke 10:18. "I beheld Satan as lightning fall from heaven."

We are given indication in other verses (Revelation 12:4; Jude 6) that the devil carried with him a whole host of angels. There is in the world a vast unseen horde of demons—devil angels, if you please, who do the bidding of the devil. He was cast out of heaven as a rebel and he took others with him. When the devil was cast out of heaven, Isaiah 14:17 indicates he was cast into the earth. "That made the world as a wilderness."

C. A Condemned Being

God has pronounced his condemnation on the devil and declared that eventually he will be cast into hell. Meanwhile, the devil has retained some authority and power. Jesus said in John 12:31 that the devil is the prince of this world. In Ephesians 2:2 Paul tells us that the devil is the prince of the power of the air.

The devil does have a certain authority. He does have temporary power, but God has pronounced judgment on him. Genesis 3:15 contains the first gospel message ever preached. God declared that there was going to be hostility between the devil's seed and the seed of woman, the promised messiah. God declared that the day would come that the woman's seed, the Son of God, would bruise the head of the serpent. Since that time there has been hostility and animosity between the devil and God.

The word *devil* is the Greek *diabolos*, which means to separate or shatter. So we see that the job of the devil is to separate humankind from God. If the devil can, he will separate you from God. He will drag you down into hell itself and see that you never enter into God's heaven.

II. THE OPERATION OF THE DEVIL

It is important to understand something of the works of the devil, the deeds of the devil, how the devil operates. We are told in Ephesians 6:11 that we are to be aware of the wiles of the devil. In 2 Corinthians 2:11 we are warned of the devices of the devil. We are taught in 2 Timothy 2:26 that the devil has snares or traps. In 1 Peter 5:8 scripture declares, "Be sober, be vigilant; because your adversary the devil, as a roaring lion, walketh about, seeking whom he may devour." We need to be forearmed against the strategies, the subtleties, and deceptive methods of the devil.

A. Mentally

The devil attacks us mentally. The devil wants our mind. He seeks to destroy people's minds through error. God confronts the mind of man with truth. John 17:17 says, "Thy word is truth." God wants his truth to get possession of our mind. If the promises and truths of God can become real in our mind and can be absorbed in our soul, our life will be different; we will never again be the same. But the devil seeks to get our mind by the intrusion of error. John 8:44 tells us that the devil is a liar from the beginning. There is no truth in him; every time he speaks, he speaks a lie. He is the father of lies.

Every time we hear something that is not true, every time we hear something contrary to God's truth as revealed in the Bible, we can be sure that the ultimate source of that untruth is the devil. If the devil can cause us to believe his lies, he has gone a long way toward wrecking our life.

That is what he did in the garden of Eden. God had already given his truth to Adam and Eve. Then the devil came with his lies. He started with doubt of the word of God; that is always the way it starts. If the devil can get you to doubt God's word, if the devil can just raise a question mark in your mind about the word of God, he has an in-road into your soul.

Many churches have swallowed the devil's lies and have raised doubts about the word of God. They have undercut the source of authority, and young people are taught that there are no absolute rights and wrongs, there is no absolute truth, there is no absolute error. So it really does not matter how you live. Live any way and it will be all right. That is why we are in the mess we are in.

Next, the devil moves on to denial of the word of God: "Ye shall not surely die." Eve rejected God's truth in her mind, accepting the devil's error. When she did, sin came into her life; she was brought into mental slavery. That is the way the devil operates. He sows the seeds of doubt and denial in your mind.

We must be careful of the things we allow to get into our mind. I have talked with many young people who use drugs. I have talked to many who have moral problems, and almost without exception these young people have been brainwashed, bombarded with the hellish lies of the devil through rock music. Parents, if you allow rock music in your home, wisdom has fled from you. It is absolutely subverting the minds of our children. They are taught to hate parents and other authority figures. They are taught to rebel against the government. They are taught to laugh at the standards of purity and chastity taught in the word of God. No wonder our young people are so mixed up. They have swallowed the devil's lies. He has attacked them mentally.

B. Morally

The devil also attacks us morally. He wants our heart. The devil wants to make us love those things we ought to hate and hate those things we ought to love. Our heart was made to love Jesus.

I have never seen a little boy or girl who did not love Jesus. I have gone into thousands of homes and talked to the children. I have said to them, "Do you love Jesus?" They look up and smile and say yes, because something about the human heart was made to love the Lord Jesus Christ.

The devil attacks us morally. The devil will seek to replace the love of Jesus in our heart with the love of sin. He does it by making sin attractive and alluring. He uses the pleasures of sin to enslave us. If the devil can cause us to love sin, he will get his foothold in our heart and before long we will be in moral slavery.

C. Motivationally

The devil also wants to take our will. Second Timothy 2:26 talks about the snare of the devil and being taken captive by him at his will. You see, the devil has a will for us. He has a plan for our life just as God does. The devil lays his trap. His purpose is to trap our will and bring it into subjection to his will. For this reason all sin is addictive.

All sin is habit-forming. We see this vividly in alcohol. Alcohol can enslave a person's will. Although we know that drugs are addictive, the government is softening its position on marijuana. That does not surprise me. That crowd in Washington so often is soft on things which are morally wrong. I have never talked to any young person hooked on any kind of drug who did not start with marijuana. Marijuana quits giving you a kick and you move to something a little stronger; then that quits giving you a kick and before long you are mainlining. The devil takes possession of your will and you are a slave to drugs. You cannot quit. The power of the devil has you.

All sin is addictive. Lying is addictive. When we lie we surrender our will to the will of the devil. Finally lying becomes habitual.

A lot of people are addicted to the love of money. When you put money ahead of God, you allow the devil to capture your will. The motivating desire of your life is to make money. It will drive you to destruction.

Loose living is habit-forming. Start playing loose with your morals, start playing loose with things God says ought to be sacred, pure, and holy, and sin will possess you.

James 1:14–15 talks about how the devil catches people. They are tempted when they are drawn away by their own lust and enticed. The devil is a smart fisherman. He knows exactly what bait to use. Some people are so gullible that all the devil has to do is just dangle a little worm in front of them and they will swallow it hook, line, and sinker. Others are more difficult. The devil knows he cannot get them with a simple red worm so he uses an elaborate plug. He will let you become proud. You begin to nibble on the bait. James says, "When lust hath conceived, it bringeth forth sin." The fish grabs the bait and the struggle is on. However, "Sin, when it is finished, bringeth forth death." The fish is thrown on the bank and it is hooked. That is the way the devil wants to do you in.

One of the most tragic examples of the methods of the devil is the life of Judas Iscariot. In John 12:3–5 a woman came to lavish her love on the Lord Jesus by pouring ointment on his feet. Judas said, "Why such waste?" This was a mental attack. John 13:2 says that Satan put it in Judas' heart to betray Jesus—a moral attack. He got Judas' heart. Finally, John 13:27 says Satan entered him. He took over his will—a motivational coup.

When Satan had Judas' mind, heart, and will, he drove him to destruction. On one occasion when Jesus cast out devils they begged him to let them go into some nearby swine. They took possession of the swine and they ran down the cliff, violently plunging into the sea. The purpose of the devil is to get possession of your life, make you believe his lies, love sin, and capture your will. He will make you like a man in an airplane who has no power whatever over the direction of the plane. It plunges down toward the mountains and there is not a thing he can do about it.

III. The Overthrow of the Devil

When I was a boy, I used to go to cowboy movies. At the end of the movies it would seem that the bad guys were going to get the good guys. The situation appeared desperate, and then all of a sudden here came the main hero. When we saw that the good guy was going to win, we would all jump up and cheer. That is the way I feel when I get to this scripture, "For this purpose the Son of God was manifested, that he might destroy the works of the devil" (1 John 3:8).

A. Commenced by Jesus

The overthrow of the devil was commenced by Jesus himself. When Jesus was born, the devil tried to have him killed, but God preserved his Son. At the temptation of Jesus, the devil sought to take him over mentally, morally, and motivationally. Yet the Lord Jesus Christ met the devil head on and when it was over the Bible says the devil left him. Jesus quoted the word of God. He used the sword of the Spirit and thus was victorious over the devil.

One day the Lord went to a final, decisive battle up Golgotha's hill. All the forces of evil, all the powers of the devil, thought they had him. When the blood poured out of the Lord Jesus Christ and his body was put in a tomb, they thought they had him. But Colossians 2:15 says, "And having spoiled principalities and powers, he made a shew of them openly, triumphing over them in it." The devil's Waterloo was the cross of Calvary.

The word *destroy* occurs twice in relation to the devil. Hebrews 2:14 says that Jesus Christ through death might destroy him that had the power of death. Then, as has been noted, 1 John 3:8 says he was manifested that he might destroy the works of the devil. Two different Greek words are used. The first word, in Hebrews 2:14, means to put out of operation or out of business. When Jesus died on the cross, the devil was put out of business. God took the stinger out of the devil at the cross. The devil is out of operation. But in 1 John 3:8, when it says he destroyed the works of the devil, the verb used means to disassemble or disintegrate.

The best illustration I can think of is a liquor still. When the revenue agents find a liquor still they do two things. First, they put the moonshiner out of business. Next they disassemble the liquor still itself. When Jesus Christ went to the cross he did two things. He put the devil out of the tempting business unless we allow him to tempt us. As far as Christians are concerned, the devil does not have any more power over us than we let him have. Jesus also started disassembling the devil's equipment, disintegrating it and disrupting his affairs.

B. Continued by the Saints

The overthrow of the devil is continued by the child of God. Romans 16:20 says, "The God of peace shall bruise Satan under your feet shortly." You can have victory over the devil. You do not have to be trampled under by the devil. You can trample him under. God has made provision for you to get victory over the devil. When the devil tempts you, you have one of two choices. You can either "give place to the devil" (Ephesians 4:27) or you can "resist the devil" (James 4:7). If you resist, God says the devil will flee from you. You can resist him on the basis of Revelation 12:11, "They overcame him by the blood of the Lamb, and by the word of their testimony."

C. Consummated at the Final Judgment

The devil knows he is a goner. As a child I thought the devil had on a red union suit, had horns and a forked tail, and went running around with a pitchfork scaring little kids. I thought the devil was in hell and from time to time would come up out of hell. The facts are, however, the devil has never been to hell. But one of these days God will throw him into hell, and the devil knows it. That is why Revelation 12:12 says that on this earth he has great wrath because he knows he has only a short time.

Why the increase in demon activity? Why the worship of Satan? I will tell you why. The devil knows that his days are numbered. He wants to drag as many human beings into hell with him as he possibly can. Revelation 20:10 says the devil will be cast into the lake of fire and brimstone, with the false prophet and the beast, and he is going to be tormented night and day forever and ever. I can hardly wait. I am going to get a grandstand seat in glory. When the Lord Jesus lays hold on the devil, I am going to shout, "Get him, Jesus, get him!" When he throws him into the lake of fire, I am going to cheer, "Hurrah for Jesus! Thank you, Jesus!"

12

Where Love Cannot Be
1 John 3:11–18

I. MURDER
   A. Where?
   B. What?
   C. Why?
II. MALICE
   A. Presence
   B. Peril
III. MISERLINESS
   A. Reflect
   B. Reject

THE THEME OF THIS PORTION OF 1 JOHN IS LOVE. OVER AND OVER WE ARE RE-minded that we are to love the Lord with all our heart, and we are to love one another. One of the assurances we have that we really are the children of God is the fact that there is genuine love in our heart for those around us, and for those who are our brothers and sisters.

I want to approach this matter of love for one another from a different point of view in this chapter. In this passage the theme of love for one another is cast in a rather negative vein; John shows us what love is not and where love cannot be.

I. Murder

Murder is the opposite of love. If there is love, there is the desire to do good and to help other people. If there is hate in our
heart, if there is murder, then we do everything we can to elimi-
nate a person. John uses an example from the Old Testament of
the first murderer to show us what murder is.

I want to ask three questions about Cain and see how the
word of God answers them in these verses (1 John 3:11–12).

A. Where?

Where did Cain come from? Look at verse 12. "Not as Cain,
who was of that wicked one. . . ." When we read Genesis 4, we
discover that Cain was born to Adam and Eve, the first man and
woman who ever lived. Also in that home was born another
son, Abel. Those two boys, Cain and Abel, had the same mother
and father, yet they were very different in their attitude and action. Why was Cain so different from his brother? John says
Cain was of the "wicked one."

That statement explodes one of the popular theories of our
day. There are many who say that all people are the children of
God, that God is the father of all persons everywhere, and
therefore we are all brothers and sisters in the same family. This
doctrine of the universal fatherhood of God and the brother-
hood of man is not taught in the word of God. First John 3:10
says, "In this the children of God are manifest, and the children
of the devil." Spiritually speaking, there are two families in this
world. Cain and Abel were of the same family physically, but
they were of different families spiritually. Cain was of his father, the devil.

All people fall into one of two categories. You are either in the
family of God and are a child of God or you are in the family of
the devil and are a child of the devil. So who was Cain? Cain
was of the "wicked one." In John 8:44 the Lord Jesus reflects the
same idea when he says, "Ye are of your father the devil, and the
lusts of your father ye will do." Cain in his attitudes and actions
originated from the devil.

B. What?

What did Cain do? Cain killed his brother. The biblical word *slew* means to put to death by violence. It means to butcher, to kill a person by cutting his throat.

In Genesis 4:8 we read these words: "And Cain talked with Abel his brother: and it came to pass, when they were in the field, that Cain rose up against Abel his brother, and slew him." He spilled the blood of his own brother on the ground.

In verse 9 the Lord came and said, "Where is Abel thy brother?"

Cain said, "I know not. Am I my brother's keeper?"

In verse 10 God said to him, "What hast thou done? the voice of thy brother's blood crieth unto me from the ground."

The blood of his brother was crying out in accusation of Cain. In Jude 11 the Bible tells us of those who "have gone in the way of Cain." With that first murder Cain began something that has multiplied through the centuries.

We are living in a world in which murder is rampant. Pick up any newspaper and it is entirely possible you will read the story of another violent murder. The murders perpetrated on this earth are extremely brutal and senseless.

C. Why?

Why did Cain do it? What caused this man to take the life of his brother? John gives us the answer in verse 12: "Because his own works were evil, and his brother's righteous." It seems that Cain and Abel had a disagreement about religion. God had given the commandment, I am quite sure, to Adam and Eve as to how they were to approach him. God prefigured the cross to Adam and Eve when he killed the animals and clothed the two of them with animal skins. They saw that the only approach to God was by the shedding of blood. They had to put their faith in the shedding of the blood; we put our faith in the shed blood of the Savior who was to come.

Cain did not want to go God's way. He wanted to make up his own religion, so he brought an offering of the fruit of the ground. He offered that to God, and it was without blood.

God will not accept our attempts to save ourselves. But how many people think they can get to heaven by what they do? You talk to people and witness to them and try to win them to faith in the Lord, and you ask them, "Do you know Christ as your Savior?" "Are you a Christian?" "Are you going to heaven when you die?" They will tell you all kinds of things. "Well, I belong to such and such a church. I am a member of that church." As if that would get anyone to heaven. Or they say, "Well, I am a pretty good fellow. I live better than a lot of people I know," or "I live better than the hypocrites in the church or the TV preachers"—as if living better than hypocrites or televangelists would get anyone to heaven. People try to get to heaven their own way, but there is only one way, the blood-sprinkled way.

There is only one entrance into heaven and that is through faith in the Lord Jesus Christ. Hebrews 11:4 says, "By faith Abel offered unto God a more excellent sacrifice than Cain." By faith he took God at his word, he went the way of the cross, so to speak, and God accepted him.

When Cain's attempt at salvation was rejected by God, when God would not accept his offering, the Bible teaches us that the envy and jealousy in his heart brought forth murder. He rejected God's offer of repentance. He rejected God's offer of mercy, and murder came into his heart. In 1 John 3:11–12 we see that love cannot be where there is murder.

II. MALICE

Are you the reader feeling rather comfortable at this point? We know the word of God says, "Thou shalt not kill," and I doubt that any of you have committed actual physical murder. If you have, let me say a word to you. It is not possible for a murderer to get to heaven, but it is possible for God to forgive you of the sin of murder, to cleanse your heart of that sin, and by the new birth make a new creature out of you and let you into heaven. Paul was a murderer. Paul had put men to death for their faith in the Lord Jesus Christ, and yet on that day when the love of God was revealed to him, God forgave him for the sin of murder. Jesus came into his life, making him over again.

Suppose you and I say, "I'm O.K. I know there can be love in my life since there is no murder in my life." But I want you to see a second thing. Love cannot be where there is malice. Where there is hatred, where there is malice in the heart, then love cannot be.

A. Presence

"Marvel not, my brethren, if the world hate you" (1 John 3:13). There we have the presence of hate in the world. John is acknowledging that we live in a world of hate. He is correct.

There is hatred between the nations of the world. One nation fights against another nation. The nations of the world are engaged in turmoil, animosity, and strife.

There is hatred in the business world. There is fierce competition. There is such a desire to succeed in business that there develops absolute hate for persons in competing industries.

There is hate between individuals. I hear people say, "I hate him! I cannot stand him! I don't want to be in the same place with that person!" If God really revealed what was in the depths of your heart, would there be hatred for another person?

On the other hand, John says we are not to be surprised when this world hates us. Why should the world hate us?

I remember when it first dawned on me that not everybody liked me. I thought they would. I could not see why everybody wouldn't like me, lovable and sweet and kind and gentle as I am! I became pastor of a Baptist church at the age of eighteen, and I thought everybody was going to love me. I thought everybody was going to be glad I had given my life to preach the gospel. Then one day I got the news that somebody did not like me. I will tell you I went home, threw myself across the bed, and wept.

The closer you get to Jesus, the more like Jesus you are in this world, the more this world is going to be uneasy around you, is going to be disturbed by you, and the more the devil is going to try to hinder you.

Jesus was put to death because he was hated. What had Jesus ever done to anybody? Nothing but good. He never did anything wrong. What sin had Jesus ever committed? Those who were downhearted could get an encouraging word from him, and their heart could be uplifted. Those who were crippled were touched by him and they could walk again. Those who needed to know the way to heaven could hear him speak and he would tell them how to get from earth to glory. The only thing Jesus Christ did was to live such a perfect life that this world could not stand it.

So we Christians ought not to be shocked or upset when the world hates us. In John 15:18 Jesus said, "It hated me before it hated you."

Then John drops another idea in the middle of this section on hate. "We know [there is some assurance] that we have passed from death unto life, because we love the brethren" (1 John 3:14). One of the ways I know I am a Christian, one of the ways I know I have made the great transfer from the land of death into the land of life, is the presence of love in my heart. The Bible describes lost persons in Titus 3:3 by saying that they are hateful and hating one another. I know I am a child of God because Jesus has put love in my heart.

If there is hatred, if there is animosity, if there is malice in your heart, the Bible says, "He that loveth not his brother abideth in death" (1 John 3:14). Love cannot coexist with hatred. The two emotions are mutually exclusive. If your heart is full of hate, then love cannot be there. If your heart is full of love, then hate cannot be there. We need to reevaluate our assurance of salvation on the basis of the terms laid down by John in these verses. One of the ways you know you are saved is that you really love other people.

B. Peril

"Whosoever hateth his brother is a murderer: and ye know that no murderer hath eternal life abiding in him" (1 John 3:15). John is warning us of the peril of hate, because hatred in one's heart is in essence equivalent to murder. In Matthew 15:19 Jesus Christ says, "For out of the heart proceed evil thoughts," and then he says "murders." The first step toward murder is to allow hatred to be in your heart. The only difference between hate and murder is the outward act; the inward attitude and intention are the same. Of course, we know it is worse for a person to murder someone than to have hatred in their heart. This is not what he is saying. He is not saying that those two acts are identical. But hatred in your heart is the moral equivalent of murder.

If you allow malice, animosity, and hatred to stay in your heart, and you nurture it, feed it, and continue to harbor it in your heart, one of these days there is the potential there for murder. If there is hate in your heart, it may be an indication you have never been born of the Spirit of God. Love cannot be where there is murder. Love cannot be where there is malice.

III. MISERLINESS

Love cannot be where there is miserliness (1 John 3:16-17). If you are a miser in your heart, love cannot be there. These two verses draw a contrast. Two examples are given: an example on which we ought to reflect, and an example that we ought to reject.

A. Reflect

"Hereby perceive we the love of God, because he [Jesus] laid down his life for us." Cain was an example of hate. Jesus is the supreme example of love. Jesus laid down his life in order to save us. In this brief statement John tells us three important things about the death of the Lord Jesus.

First, Jesus' death was voluntary. He laid down his life. In John 10 Jesus tells about the good shepherd and says, "I am the good shepherd: the good shepherd giveth his life for the sheep." In John 10:17 Jesus says, "Therefore doth my Father love me, because I lay down my life, that I might take it again." And in John 10:18, "No man taketh it from me, but I lay it down of myself."

Unless Jesus Christ had decided to die on the cross, he never would have died. When Jesus died on the cross he said, "Father, into thy hands I commend my spirit" (Luke 23:46). The Bible says he "gave up the ghost." Jesus Christ was no martyr on that cross. I have heard people compare the Lord Jesus Christ to martyrs or compare him to those whose life was taken from them accidentally. But Jesus came into this world for the purpose of laying down his life. His death was voluntary.

Second, his death was vicarious; it was a death on behalf of others. He laid down his life for us, and the preposition *for* is important. It means "in the place of," "instead of," and the implication is clear. The death of Jesus Christ was substitutionary.

A substitute is someone who goes into a football or basketball game for someone else. Number 56 is going in for Number 52. He is a substitute. That is what this verse is teaching us. We perceive the love of God in that he laid down his life for us, in place of us, in our stead, as our substitute.

Jesus Christ on that cross became all of your sin. Every sin you ever committed, Jesus Christ became on the cross. The wages of sin are death, and when Jesus Christ was "made sin" for this world, God punished our sins in his person. He took our place. He died for us. His death was vicarious.

Third, his death was victorious. Verb tenses, especially in 1 John, are crucial, and the tense of the verb here, "laid down," means a once-for-all action. Revelation 1:5 says, "Unto him that loved us . . ." That verb should be translated as present tense; its action goes on and on. He will never stop loving us; his love is a continual love, an eternal love. There was never a time when God did not love us. There will never be a time in the future when God does not love us. Right now in every moment of our life, God loves us. The second verb in Revelation 1:5 is "washed us" from our sin. There John uses a different tense meaning "once for all." Likewise here in 1 John 3:16 it says he laid down his life for us, once for all. When Jesus died on the cross, he exclaimed in triumph, "It is finished!" His death was victorious.

The Son of God laid down his life to save us, and we ought to lay down our life to serve him. The tense of the verb here is present tense—not a once-for-all kind of service, not something you do at Thanksgiving because you feel especially grateful, not something you do at Christmas because you feel especially spiritual or especially compassionate toward other people. John is saying that our daily attitude, the daily disposition of our life ought to be that we lay down our life in service for people. Our life ought to be constantly lived for others. That is the only way we will come to fulfillment, joy, and meaning in life.

I have great admiration for The Salvation Army. Those dear people have probably done as much to live out the claims of Jesus Christ in daily matters as any group I know. William Booth was expected to come to a great convocation of The Salvation Army and at the last minute he could not come. They wired

him: "General Booth, send us a message to challenge us." A day
or so of the convocation passed, and they did not hear from him.
Finally, the telegram came. When they opened it, it said: "Others." What Booth meant by that one-word message was: Lord,
help me to live for others that I might live for thee. Jesus said,
"Inasmuch as ye have done it unto one of the least of these my
brethren, ye have done it unto me" (Matthew 25:40). We are
called to reflect his kind of love.

B. Reject

John also gives us an example to reject, the example of a
miser. "But whoso hath this world's good. . . ." He means whoever has what sustains life, whoever has the necessities of life—
food and clothing and shelter. He is talking to us, is he not? He is
not talking to the millionaires of the world. He is not talking to
those who are financially independent. He is talking to those of
us who have the necessities. Do you have food on your table? He
is talking to you. Do you have clothing on your back? He is talking to you. Do you have shelter, a warm house to live in? He is
talking to you. "Whoso hath this world's good, and seeth his
brother have need. . . ."

Jesus Christ was drawn to human need like metal shavings to
a magnet. When Jesus saw a need, he had to do something about
it. How many times we are told that Jesus was moved with compassion and then did something to alleviate human need. So,
John says, here you are a Christian, you have the necessities of
life, and you see someone who has a need. ". . . and shutteth up
his bowels of compassion from him. . . ." John is saying that if
someone else has a need and you lock the door on your compassion, if you refuse to let your heart go out in positive action, then
you'd better start to wonder if you truly have the love of God in
your heart.

In the parable of the Good Samaritan, a man was taken by
thieves down that winding Jericho Road. What a road that is—
desolate, dark, alone. The poor man on the way down to Jericho
fell among thieves, and they beat him and stripped him and
wounded him and left him for dead. A Levite came by, and he
saw him, and when he saw his need, he locked up his compassion and walked off. A priest came by and had enough interest

to go over and look at him, and he saw his need, but he too locked up his compassion and walked off. James said there are those who will say to people who are hungry and naked, "Be fed; Be clothed." What good does it do to say things and not do things? We talk about soulwinning and we talk and talk and talk about it. What good does it do if we never do anything about it? We talk about helping the needy and alleviating the plight of the poor, the suffering, and the hungry. What good does it do to talk about such things and not do something about them?

Then the Good Samaritan came by and had compassion on the wounded man. He got right down in the ditch with him, poured in the healing oil, bound up his wounds, put him on his animal, and carried him to a place of lodging. Further, he told the innkeeper, "I am going to pay his bill, and when I come back, if he has incurred any more expenses, I will stand good for them." That is New Testament love. John says, If you do not have that kind of love, how can the love of God be in you?

"My little children, let us not love in word, neither in tongue: but in deed and in truth" (1 John 3:18). James 1:22 says, "Be ye doers of the word, and not hearers only."

These words that John gives us about love are not to be just heard, they are to be carried out in our daily life, lived out in our daily experience.

13

The Cure for an
Accusing Heart
1 John 3:19–24

I. ASSURANCE
  A. A Condemning Heart
  B. A Confident Heart
II. ANSWERED PRAYER
  A. Blessing
  B. Basis
III. ABIDING
  A. We Abide in Him
  B. He Abides in Us

IN THE THIRD CHAPTER OF 1 JOHN WE HAVE SEEN SOME THINGS THAT WILL HIN-
der our enjoyment of the love of God. In the last verses of
chapter 3, John brings up another hindrance to our enjoyment of the love of God, an accusing heart. In John 14:27 the
Lord says, "Peace I leave with you, my peace I give unto you: not
as the world giveth, give I unto you. Let not your heart be troubled, neither let it be afraid." The birthright of every child of
God is peace, tranquility, and calmness of heart. Why is it that

the majority of Christians do not enjoy the peace of God, and therefore do not enjoy the love of God?

I suppose if there were some way for us to determine it, we would discover that there are as many Christians who spend their money on tranquilizers and other things trying to find peace and calmness in their life as those who are not Christian. God has given us his peace as a legacy, but clearly many Christians do not experience the peace of God. One of the common problems, I believe, of average Christians is this matter of an accusing heart. I want to consider the cure for such a heart.

I. Assurance

"And hereby we know that we are of the truth, and shall assure our hearts before him" (1 John 3:19). Let us study that word *assure* for a moment. It means to persuade, soothe, tranquilize. John is describing the condition of heart that God intends every Christian to have. It is not good for Christians to go through life never sure of where they really stand with God, never sure about their relationship to him, and whether or not they are on speaking terms with him. It is possible for us to have assurance of heart rather than an accusing heart. We can have an experience "before him" that is personal and intimate.

A. A Condemning Heart

Two conditions of heart are dealt with in this section, a condemning heart and a confident heart. "For if our heart condemn us ..." (1 John 3:20). The word *condemn* suggests ideas like if our heart blames us, if our heart finds fault with us, if our heart puts us down.

Christians have to face this in our own experience. We each know ourselves better than any other person knows us. We each know the deepest thoughts of our heart. We know our relationship to other people and our relationship to God. If we do not read the Bible as we should, we are the first to realize it. If prayer is not as important as it ought to be in our life, we are the first to know it. If we are not witnessing as God intends, our heart is aware of this. The more we grow as a Christian, the

more sensitive we become to our own spiritual condition and to
what God expects us to be.

As we read the New Testament, we see God's standard for us
and how far short we fall. So, if we are serious as Christians, if
we are sincere, we are plagued with the problem of an accusing
heart. Our heart makes us aware of our failures as children of
God. This condition of the heart, the condemning heart, can be
very detrimental in our life if we do not come to grips with it in
the word of God.

How is it possible for us to move from having a condemning
heart to a confident heart? What is the cure for this malady?

B. A Confident Heart

In 1 John 3:20 we find a twofold cure for an accusing heart.
John says that God is greater than our heart. What he is saying
is this. When we have the problem of an accusing heart, as we
confess our sin to God and put it under the blood of the Lord
Jesus Christ, we are then to turn our attention from the greatness of our sin and failure to the greatness of the mercy and
love of God. God is merciful toward us in spite of our sins. We
are not saved because we are "goody-goody," because we deserve to be saved. God did not look down on the world and say,
"I am going to find the best people I can, and I am going to save
them." No, "Christ Jesus came into this world to save sinners."
He came because we were sinners, because we were in the
depths of sin. Because God is a God of mercy, it is possible for
us to be saved. We look not to the greatness of our sin, but to the
great mercy of God.

In the Old Testament Israel worshiped in a building known as
the tabernacle, and we find a number of instructive pictures
about our Christian life in tabernacle symbolism. In the holy of
holies, for instance, there was a piece of furniture known as the
ark of the covenant. In it, among other things, were tablets of
stone inscribed with the ten commandments. Those stones re-
minded the people of Israel of their failure before God, that they
deserved the wrath of God against their sin.

In that holy of holies the ark of the covenant was not left ex-
posed to view. On top of it was a slab made of pure gold, known
as the mercy seat, which completely covered the ark. It was as

long as the ark was long. It was as wide as the ark was wide. It was the exact dimensions of the ark because it was intended to illustrate the truth that however great our sins are, the grace and mercy of God are just as great, just as wide.

In Psalm 103:10–12 we have a statement about the mercy of God. "He hath not dealt with us after our sins; nor rewarded us according to our iniquities. For as the heaven is high above the earth, so great is his mercy toward them that fear him. As far as the east is from the west, so far hath he removed our transgressions from us." One dimension of the mercy seat, however, was never given. We are never told its thickness. Do you know why? That illustrates the truth that the mercy of God is high enough, deep enough, to meet us in whatever are the depths of our own experience.

We can rejoice in the truth that God does not deal with us in harshness. God does not judge us wrongly nor severely, but rather on the basis of his mercy. The first cure for an accusing heart is the greatness of the mercy of God.

Second, still referring to God, John says, " . . . and knoweth all things." God is omniscient. There is not a thing you can teach God. God has never learned anything; if God had to learn something, he would not have been God before he had to learn it. God has never forgotten anything; if God had forgotten some knowledge, then he would cease to be God. No gossiper can inform God about us. No enemy can dig up some hidden knowledge that God does not know about us. God knows where you were last night. He knows what you did last week. He knows what you are thinking right now. He knows what you are planning to do tomorrow. God knows your past, present, and future. There is no escaping the eyes of a God who knows everything. That ought to be alarming if you are not right with God.

However, there is also comfort in the fact that God knows your heart. Regardless of your faith, or how far short you may be of what God intends for you to be, you can rest and soothe your heart in the truth that God understands your true desire.

Sometimes I see how far short I fall. I see my failure as a Christian and as a preacher, and my heart condemns me. My heart puts me down and says, "Why, you are not worthy to be a Christian." My heart then has to look up to God and say, "O God, thou knowest all things. Thou knowest my heart." In that experience

I find the cure for an accusing heart. I find then that I can have a confident heart, not because I am worthy nor because I deserve it, but I rest my soul on his mercy and omniscience. He knows all things. We can have confidence toward God because we are resting in a God who is greater than our sin.

II. ANSWERED PRAYER

A second truth relates to this matter, and it is answered prayer (1 John 3:22). Here we see the blessing of answered prayer and also the basis of answered prayer.

A. Blessing

"And whatsoever we ask, we receive of him." What a sweeping statement about the blessing of prayer. Why, that is like a blank check! What a definition of prayer! Prayer is going to God and asking for definite things. Do you know the reason we do not get more answers from God in prayer? It is because we are not definite enough in our prayers. James said in chapter 4 of his book, "Ye have not, because ye ask not."

We could have a lot more from God if we would just ask. "Ask, and it shall be given you; seek, and ye shall find; knock, and it shall be opened unto you" (Matthew 7:7). What a picture of prayer. Jesus promises us that if we ask, God will give to us.

B. Basis

A condition is attached to this promise. We will get what we ask if we are keeping his commandments and doing those things that are pleasing to him.

Suppose tomorrow your child is rebellious and stubborn. He resists everything you say to him. Suppose after all his rebellion and disobedience he comes in to ask you for something. How would you feel? Would you be anxious to do it? Would you be anxious to grant it? That is the way God is. If we have a listening ear to his commandments, God says he will have a listening ear to our requests in prayer. We must pour over his word. We must study his word, find what God commands us to do, and do it. Then we get on praying ground and we can talk to God.

Although some things are not specifically commanded in the Bible, the sincere Christian will not only keep the commandments of God, but will find out the things that please the Lord and do those things too (Psalm 37:4).

Incidentally, this is a good place to help you solve the question of right and wrong. Ask yourself about any matter you are considering: Does it please Jesus? Would Jesus be pleased if I did this? Would Jesus be pleased with this course of action? Would Jesus be pleased with the activity? Those questions will settle a lot of problems about right and wrong.

III. Abiding

The last verse in 1 John 3 mentions "abiding": "he that keepeth his commandments dwelleth in him."

A. We Abide in Him

We abide in the Lord. We have the privilege of being in fellowship with the Lord. As we study his word and as we pray, we abide in him.

B. He Abides in Us

Then John turns it around and says that abiding is a reciprocal relationship. We abide in him, and he, the Lord, abides in us. He comes to live with us. He has fellowship with us. In Revelation 3:20, the Lord says: "Behold, I stand at the door, and knock: if any man hear my voice, and open the door, I will come in to him, and will sup with him, and he with me."

In Luke 24 Jesus had been raised from the dead. Two of his disciples were on the road to Emmaus, and Jesus went with them. When it was about time for the sun to go down, they came to their place of dwelling and said to Jesus, "Come in and abide with us." So he went in at their invitation and a wonderful thing took place. The one who was invited to be their guest became the host. He took the bread, broke it, and served it to them. When you invite Christ into your life he takes over and becomes the host. He meets the problems of your heart.

How can we know that the Lord is in our heart? How do you

know Jesus is there? "And hereby we know that he abideth in us, by the Spirit which he hath given us." When you become a Christian, the Holy Spirit of God comes into your life. John 7:37–38 says, "If any man thirst, let him come unto me, and drink . . . out of his belly shall flow rivers of living water." Then John says in verse 39, "This spake he of the Spirit, which they that believe on him should receive." First Corinthians 6:19–20 says, "Know ye not that your body is the temple of the Holy Ghost which is in you?" Romans 8:9 says, "Now if any man have not the Spirit of Christ, he is none of his." So, when you receive Christ as your Savior, the Spirit of God comes to dwell in your heart, and from time to time the Holy Spirit supernaturally, mystically, makes himself known in your heart, lets you know that you are his.

Let me tell you how the Holy Spirit of God made himself real in my heart. I received Jesus when I was nine years old. I am so glad I did. (Parents ought to pray for the conversion of their children at an early age. You had better get them saved and under the blood early, before this world has time to twist them and turn them away from the things of Jesus.) For several years, however, I did not grow in my Christian life. I did not mature. I did not study the Bible and I did not really become what God wanted me to be.

At the age of sixteen, because of some things in my life, I became greatly disturbed about my spiritual condition. My heart accused me and justly so, because there was little in my life that should have been there as a born-again child of God. I began to study the Bible and God dealt with me. I began to wonder, "Am I really a Christian? Do I really know Jesus as my Savior?" Finally, I could stand it no more. I had read what the Bible said a person had to do to become a Christian. I had read that you have to repent of sin and put your faith in the Lord Jesus. You must invite him by faith to come into your heart. I got on my knees by the side of my bed and I said, "Lord, I am not sure I am a Christian. My heart accuses me because of my life. If I am not really a Christian, dear Lord, I want to be one right now." I did not hear any bells clanging or see any lights flashing. I did not hear an audible voice, but the Holy Spirit of God seemed to say to me down deep in my soul, "Jerry, you do not need to do that. You have already done that. You have already accepted Jesus as your

Savior. What you need to do now is commit your life anew to me and let me take over." In that moment assurance came. I made the glad transition from a condemning heart to a confident heart.

To this very day I have never seriously doubted that I am a child of God. Do you have that assurance? Do you know that in spite of the failures of your life and in spite of an accusing heart, Jesus Christ is your Savior? You can have that assurance now.

14

Truth and Error
1 John 4:1–6

I. FALSE PROPHETS
   A. Content
   B. Congeniality
   C. Commercialism
   D. Character
   E. Converts
II. FAITHFUL PREACHERS
   A. Agreement with the Bible
   B. Acceptance by Believers
III. FEARLESS PEOPLE
   A. Relationship
   B. Result
   C. Reason

AT THIS POINT IN HIS LETTER JOHN GIVES US A WARNING THAT WILL FORtify us against the danger of spiritual gullibility. Christians are not to accept everything they hear as the truth, even though what they hear may come from supposedly Christian sources.

John contrasts the spirit of truth and the spirit of error. This lets us know that behind the world we perceive with our senses, there is a real, unseen world. In Ephesians 6:12 we read, "For we wrestle not against flesh and blood, but against principalities, against powers, against the rulers of the darkness of this world, against spiritual wickedness in high places." In that spirit world a titanic struggle goes on between the forces of good and the forces of evil. There is a spirit of truth which is of God, and there is a spirit of error which is of the devil.

It is the purpose of God to confront humankind with truth. God changes and directs our life as we respond to his infallible truth. It is the purpose of the devil to confront us with error and thus to enslave us. So it is possible for someone to be possessed by the Spirit of God and to preach the truth of God, and it is also possible for someone to be possessed by the spirit of error and to preach what is untrue.

We must apply the proper spiritual tests to the things we hear. It is important to teach our children how to eat properly; we would not think of suggesting that they indiscriminately take anything into their mouth without prior examination. The same thing is true concerning the things we hear. We must be careful to discover whether they are of the truth or whether they are of error.

John says that we are not to believe every spirit, but to try the spirits whether they are of God (1 John 4:1). The word translated "try" could be translated "test" or "prove." In Bible days the word was used with reference to putting metals to the test to see if they were genuine. You and I are commanded in the word of God to apply spiritual tests to the things we hear. Acts 17:11 says, "These [the Christians in Berea] were more noble than those in Thessalonica, in that they received the word with all readiness of mind, and searched the scriptures daily, whether those things were so." In 1 Thessalonians 5:21–22 we are told, "Prove all things: hold fast that which is good. Abstain from all appearance of evil."

How do we put things to the test? How do we discover whether or not they are of God?

Three personal pronouns are used successively in 1 John 4:4–6. Verse 4 says, " *Ye* are of God." Verse 5 says, "*They* are of the world." Verse 6 says, "*We* are of God." In those three pronouns John has sketched for us three different groups.

I. FALSE PROPHETS

In verse 1 John says that many false prophets have gone out into the world. How much more is that true in our day.

John says in 1 John 4:5, "They are of the world: therefore speak they of the world, and the world heareth them." Jude 4 says, "For there are certain men crept in unawares." Jude is saying that false prophets and false teachers will creep unrecognized into the fellowship of God's people.

In 2 Peter 2:1 Peter says, "But there were false prophets also among the people, even as there shall be false teachers among you, who privily shall bring in damnable heresies."

The Bible warns us in many places of the encroachment of false prophets seeking to spread the spirit of error among the people of God. Our Savior predicted that false prophets would come into the world. In Matthew 7:15 Jesus says, "Beware of false prophets, which come to you in sheep's clothing, but inwardly they are ravening wolves." In Matthew 24 the Lord Jesus Christ says that there would be false prophets who will seek to deceive many (v. 11), and he continues in verse 24 of that chapter, "that, if it were possible, they shall deceive the very elect." Now, if these false prophets and teachers come in sheep's clothing, if they look like the true but in reality they are the false, if outwardly they appear as the real thing, yet inwardly they are the spirit of error, how is the child of God to know it when he or she encounters a false prophet?

John says, "Try the spirits. Examine the spirits. Put them to the test, to see if they are of God." I want to suggest several ways to test every sermon, every message you hear, to determine whether or not it is of God.

A. Content

Test number one: Check the content. John says, "And every spirit that confesseth not that Jesus Christ is come in the flesh is not of God" (1 John 4:3). False prophets will say many things that are true. However, because a person says some true things, it does not mean that he is of God and that everything he says is the truth of God. Check the content.

John says that the key question is what they teach about

Jesus. If they do not confess that Jesus is Christ come in the flesh, they are not of God. The crucial question is always this: "What do you think of Jesus Christ?" Matthew 22:42 asks, "What think ye of Christ, whose son is he?" What people think about Jesus Christ is the touchstone of correctness and truthfulness in matters of the faith. Every major cult is in error concerning the person of the Lord Jesus Christ.

In the particular time in which John was writing, there was a heresy abroad known as the Cerinthian heresy. It was a blatant denial of the deity of the Lord Jesus. The Cerinthian heresy taught that Jesus was the physical son of Joseph, and that at his baptism Jesus, who was just a man, was come upon by an aeonian, or eternal being, Christ. Christ abode in the human Jesus. When Jesus went to the cross, the divine Christ abandoned him, and Jesus died as a mere man. That heresy denies the deity of Jesus and the work he came to do in the sacrifice of Calvary.

So, here is one test: What is being taught about the Lord Jesus? False preachers will be in error concerning his birth, his blood, the Bible, and the blessed hope of his coming again.

B. Congeniality

Test number two: Check their congeniality. "They [false prophets] are of the world: therefore speak they of the world, and the world heareth them" (1 John 4:5). Check their popularity. I am not saying that popularity is proof positive that a teacher is not of God. Of course, that wouldn't be true. Many great teachers are very popular; multitudes of people come to listen to them expound the word of God. But one of the marks of an unfaithful prophet, or a false prophet, is that he appeals to the masses of the people. He is popular with this world. He is of the world. The world recognizes its own, because a false prophet teaches things that the world wants to hear.

False prophets are often smooth in their talk; they may be plausible, convincing, and attractive in their arguments. Everything about them is congenial, geared to win popular approval.

It is interesting, however, to note that virtually all false prophets, although they are congenial toward the world, are hostile and uncongenial toward the true church of the Lord

Jesus Christ. Almost without exception they attack the church. They imply that everyone who does not agree with them is a narrow-minded and ignorant fundamentalist.

C. Commercialism

Test number three: Check their commercialism. In 2 Peter 2:2–3 the Bible says, "And many shall follow their pernicious ways; by reason of whom the way of truth shall be evil spoken of. And through covetousness shall they with feigned words make merchandise of you." That is, they exploit their followers commercially.

One characteristic of false prophets is that they are constantly appealing for money. I heard a false prophet announcing that he had a miracle billfold he wanted to send to his radio audience. He told how wonderful the miracle billfold was: Why, it was just as empty as it could be, yet, he said, the Lord told him to open it, and when he did, there was a hundred-dollar bill. So he wanted to send everybody a miracle billfold. Just as soon as he made his appeal to send out miracle billfolds, he also made an appeal for money, asking people to send in offerings.

Yes, false prophets are especially interested in material gain.

D. Character

Test number four: Check their character. What kind of life do they live? Jude 4 refers to "ungodly men, turning the grace of our God into lasciviousness." False prophets use the grace of God as an excuse to sin. They rationalize sinful things in their life.

One leading speaker, who went all over this country holding meetings and making a million dollars in the process, died an alcoholic. Another man, one of the leaders of a tremendously large, modern-day false cult, was recently expelled from his own denomination by his father. However, even though he had been convicted of adultery, he was returned to his position of power in the denomination. He said, "My private life is my own business. My public life is dedicated to the Lord."

What kind of life does a particular teacher live? Does the message preached change his life and make him like the Lord Jesus Christ?

E. Converts

Test number five: Check their converts. In Matthew 7:15–16 Jesus talks about false prophets. "Ye shall know them by their fruits." One way to check the validity of someone's message is to examine the kind of converts that the message produces. Of course, all of us who are winning souls to Jesus have those who come under our ministry who do not become what God intends for them. This kind of thing is always an embarrassment to the person who preaches and teaches the word of God.

Some years ago in a city in my home state, a man who knew me was walking on the street and met up with a fellow who was so drunk he could hardly stand. He asked him, "Are you a Christian?" The man replied, "Yeah, yeah, I am one of the Jerry Vines converts." He certainly must have been one of mine; he was not one of the Lord's! There are always some individuals like that who break your heart, but I am saying this: Look at the overall character of the people who come under the ministry of a man, and you will discover if he is of God, if his ministry is of the Lord. Converts of the true man of God will tend to be Christ-exalting, Bible-believing, church-loving people.

II. FAITHFUL PREACHERS

In 1 John 4:6 John says, "We are of God." He refers to faithful preachers. How can you tell the faithful preacher of the gospel? Two specific tests are given and I will deal with just those two in this discussion.

A. Agreement with the Bible

You can tell faithful preachers by their agreement with the Bible. "Hereby know ye the Spirit of God: Every spirit that confesseth that Jesus Christ is come in the flesh is of God" (1 John 4:2). The word confess means to say the same things, or to agree with. Faithful preachers will say the same thing the Bible says. They will never raise question marks in the mind of their

hearers about the word of God; rather, they will add exclama-
tion marks to their words about the authority and inspiration of
the word of God.

Faithful preachers will be clear about the incarnation of Jesus
Christ. The incarnation of Jesus is more than the birth of the
Son of God; it includes all aspects of the coming of Jesus. The
doctrine of Christ is like the seamless robe that he wore; it is of
one piece. To rip it at any point is to damage the whole. To deny
any fundamental doctrine concerning the person and work of
the Lord Jesus Christ is to undermine the whole.

Faithful preachers will accept the virgin birth of Jesus as
taught in the Bible, the substitutionary atonement of Jesus
Christ on the cross of Calvary. They will not be ambivalent
about the inspiration of the word of God or the blessed truth
that Jesus Christ is going to come again.

Check them out. Find out if they agree with the Bible.

When I stand to preach the word of God in the pulpit, the only
authority I have is the authority derived from "Thus saith the
Lord." That is why you ought to bring your Bible. Check me out.
Put me to the test. If what I say disagrees with the Bible, then
discard what I say. It is not true. But if what I say is what the
Bible says, if what I teach is congruent with the teachings of the
word of God, then take it into your heart and live by it.

B. Acceptance by Believers

A second way to recognize faithful preachers is that they are
accepted by believers. They appeal to those who are born again.
"He that knoweth God heareth us; he that is not of God heareth
not us." John is saying that faithful preachers will get one of two
responses from a congregation. There will be those who will not
hear them. There will also be those who will. John knew what it
was to preach to a congregation and encounter the cold, indif-
ferent, hostile stares of those who do not receive the word of
God. I know what it is to preach to people who do not believe the
word of God. I know what it is for people to hear the word of God
and reject that word.

I was preaching in a church many years ago and it became obvious from the outset that one couple in the church was in-
censed by the things I had to say. I searched my heart. I asked

God if something about the manner in which I delivered my
message was offensive. I asked the Lord if anything about my
presentation of the word of God would have brought the word
into disrepute. But that was not it. It was hostility to the simplest
truths of the word of God. Soon after leaving that church, I received the sad news that the wife was having an affair with her
boss, and her husband was a homosexual. "The natural man
receiveth not the things of the Spirit of God: for they are foolishness unto him: neither can he know them, because they are
spiritually discerned" (1 Corinthians 2:14). Those who are false
will not hear, but those who are true believers will accept the
message of a true man of God.

It is wonderful to preach the word of God to people who believe in Jesus and in his word. There is a receptiveness in the
heart of the people that lets the man of God know it is being received. Something in the heart of a Christian responds to faithful proclamation of the word of God. This is why if the man of
God is really preaching, and you are a child of God, God will
send some word to your soul just when you need it. God will
give you encouragement, a word of comfort, instruction, and direction. That is how you recognize faithful preachers.

III. Fearless People

We are living in a world where there is the spirit of truth and
error. How are we to cope with this as God's people? First John
4:4 gives us wonderful encouragement. It says three things
about God's fearless people.

A. Relationship

"Ye are of God." There is a relationship. You belong to God,
and just as parents will see to it that their child is guarded from
things that are hurtful, as children of God we have a heavenly
Father who cares for us, sees to it that we understand what is
true and are able to detect what is false.

B. Result

There is a result. "You have overcome them." The tense of the verb means that something took place in the past and brings present results. We have victory in the Lord Jesus Christ. On the cross Jesus triumphed over the spiritual forces of error (Colossians 2:15). John 16:33 says, "In the world ye shall have tribulation: but be of good cheer; I have overcome the world." You and I can overcome the spirit of error in the power of the Lord Jesus.

C. Reason

How do we overcome? "Greater is he that is in you, than he that is in the world." As we have seen, in this world is the spirit of error. A multitude of false prophets promulgate damnable heresies, denying the Lord that bought them, and turning the grace of God into lasciviousness. But against that onslaught of the forces of error, God has insulated us with his Spirit. God has given us the Spirit of truth. Jesus says, "When he, the Spirit of truth, is come, he will guide you into all truth" (John 16:13). We have a divine disinfectant. We have the Spirit within us, who can protect us from heresies and false doctrines. In that assurance, in that victory, let us move into our world, launching a mighty offensive against the spirit of error. The best way to deal with it is to attack with the Spirit of truth, the word of God, the sword of the Spirit.

15

Love Is the Theme
1 John 4:7–16

I. LOVE PROCLAIMED
   A. The Nature of Our Father
   B. The Nature of Our Family
II. LOVE PROVED
   A. The Son
   B. The Satisfaction
   C. The Savior
III. LOVE PRACTICED
   A. A Commandment
   B. A Communion

THE WRITINGS OF THE APOSTLE JOHN GIVE THREE DEFINITIVE STATEMENTS about God. "God is a Spirit" (John 4:24). "God is light" (1 John 1:5). And now, twice in the present passage, "God is love" (1 John 4:8,16). The theme of everything John has to write is that our God is a God of love.

John was overwhelmed by the wonderful truth that God loved him and had proved his love by sending the Lord Jesus into the world. You know that John refers to himself in his gospel as the beloved disciple or that disciple "whom Jesus loved." The truth that really gripped his heart and meant more to him than any other was the truth that Jesus Christ loved him.

A well-known twentieth-century theologian was asked during the question-and-answer period of a huge convocation to state his theology. He replied, "Jesus loves me, this I know, for the Bible tells me so." I want everyone to understand that our God is a God of love. He loves every one of us individually.

A poet put it this way:

> "How thou canst think of us so well
> And be the God thou art
> Is darkness to my intellect
> But sunshine to my heart.

We can never take it in; we can never expound it adequately enough. We can never really go to the depths of it, but our heart can experience it and we can rejoice in it.

I. Love Proclaimed

John gives us a clear statement here about the love of God. "Love is of God, and God is love." Over and over John returns to the subject of love. He does not seem able to get away from it. Every time he mentions the love of God he goes a little deeper.

When I was a boy we used to go on camping trips. One day we decided we were going to trace a stream to its source. We started out in the early morning; we went through brush and through wilderness. All day we followed the stream until finally we came to a lovely little spring, its source. This is what John is doing as he weaves the subject of love throughout his epistle. He traces love to its source and when he arrives at the fountain-head of love he says, "Love is of God, for God is love."

A. The Nature of Our Father

When John proclaims the theme of love he first tells us something about the nature of our heavenly Father. He says, "God is love." He does not say that love is God. For John to have made a statement like that would have been to declare that God is an abstract being, an unreal being. John does not ascribe impersonal qualities or characteristics to God.

I heard about a seminary professor who was quite strong on the theme of love. One day he had the sidewalk paved in front of his home, and the cement was still wet. A little neighbor boy was playing around there and did not realize it was wet. He ran right through the concrete and messed up the sidewalk job. That teacher really railed at him. The next day his class was ready for him: "You have been telling us that we ought to love one another, yet look how hard you were on that kid." The professor replied, "It's like this, I love him in the abstract but I do not love him in the concrete." The Bible is not talking about love in the abstract. Our God is a God of love.

When John wrote these words, the concept was something new in the ancient world. Never would the people of pagan religions have declared that their god was a god of love. They would have declared that their god was a god to be feared, a god who was angry with them. It was a new thought to declare "God is love."

Study comparative religions and see what Buddhism has to say. Read what Islam has to say, all of the religions of the world, and you will discover that only the Christian gospel affirms that "God is love."

A great deal of what we call love is not really love at all. A man says he loves a girl, insists that she marry him, and she refuses him. So he takes a gun and shoots her. He says, "I did it because I loved her." That is not love. The love of God is genuine. It thinks about the loved object and not about itself. It is willing to risk itself, to be hurt, to be wounded. When John proclaims the love of God he says something about the nature of our Father.

B. The Nature of Our Family

"Love is of God; every one that loveth is born of God." Those who are children of God will be characterized by love.

People born physically take on the nature of their father and mother. We say, "Why, he is just like his dad. He is the spitting image of his father."

This is also why we are sinners. This is why we need a Savior. When we were born the first time we were born in the flesh, and our spiritual father at the first birth was none other than Adam. "Wherefore, as by one man sin entered into the world, and death by sin; and so death passed upon all men, for that all have sinned" (Romans 5:12). When we were born the first time we took on the nature of our first father and therefore we are sinners by nature and we need salvation.

When people are born the second time they take on the nature of the heavenly Father. It will therefore be characteristic of those who are children of God to live lives that are motivated by love.

You can discover if you are a member of God's family by this simple test. John says, "He that loveth not knoweth not God; for God is love" (1 John 4:8). If there is not love in your heart toward other people, you do not know God.

II. Love Proved

Love has an intangible quality. It is something you cannot touch or smell. You cannot take love, store it in a jar, and put it away for safekeeping. In order for human beings to understand his love, God had to prove that love, to manifest that love. That is exactly what he did. "In this was manifested the love of God toward us . . . . " The word *manifested* means "made visible." God wanted to prove beyond a shadow of a doubt that he loves us.

A. The Son

God proved his love to us first of all in that he sent Jesus. "In this was manifested the love of God toward us, because that God sent his only begotten Son." The word *sent* here is the word from which we get the English word *apostle*. John is saying, "God loved us so much that he sent his Son away to come into this world to be the Savior." Think about the going-away of Jesus from heaven. What a send-off Jesus must have been given as he got ready to leave the ivory palaces of glory, come down into this world, and walk as God's Son on this earth.

Jesus was God's "only begotten Son." This phrase is used in only one other context. In Hebrews 11:17 the Bible talks about Isaac, the son of Abraham. In that verse Isaac is called Abraham's "only begotten son." The word for "only begotten" means "unique, one of a kind, the only one of its kind." There had never been one like Isaac before. He was uniquely Abraham's son. Jesus came into the world in a unique way as God's only begotten Son.

Four other times in the writings of John Jesus is described as the only begotten Son. John 1:14 says, "And the Word [Jesus] was made flesh, and dwelt among us, (and we beheld his glory, the glory as of the only begotten of the Father)." The only Son, the unique Son of the Father. "We beheld his glory." When people saw Jesus they saw a revelation of God they had never seen before. "No man hath seen God at any time; the only begotten Son, which is in the bosom of the Father, he hath declared him" (John 1:18). Jesus Christ in a unique way declared the glory of God.

Now, let us consider John 3:16. "For God so loved the world, that he gave his only begotten Son, that whosoever believeth in him should not perish, but have everlasting life." And John 3:18: "He that believeth on him is not condemned: but he that believeth not is condemned already, because he hath not believed in the name of the only begotten Son of God."

Heaven was filled with amazement when Jesus came into the world. It ought to fill our heart with gratitude and praise that God loved us enough—not to send an angel, not to send some other kind of heavenly being to represent him—but to deprive himself of the fellowship of his only Son in order that he might come into this world to be the Savior.

B. The Satisfaction

"Herein is love, not that we loved God, but that he loved us" (1 John 4:10). Where does love begin? Not with us. It begins with God. It is not that we loved God, but that God loved us "and sent his Son to be the propitiation for our sins." The word *propitiation* means "satisfaction." In the English dictionary the word is defined as "appeasement" and we get the idea there that God is an emotionally volatile God who is angry with human beings, and therefore something has to be done to appease him. That is not the New Testament meaning of the word at all. It means "to satisfy God's broken law."

Hebrews 9:2–5 alludes to the tabernacle furnishings in the Old Testament. The word *mercyseat* is the same word translated in 1 John 4:10 as "propitiation." When you read "propitiation" it means "satisfaction." When you read "mercyseat" it means "the place of satisfaction." As has been noted, in the Old Testament there was an ark of the covenant. On top of the ark was placed a slab of gold, where the blood of the sacrificial lamb was poured. The Bible teaches that when God looked at the blood his holiness was satisfied.

We are told in 1 John that "God is light." God is absolutely holy and he cannot tolerate sin. We are also told that "God is love." Though we have sinned, God loves us. Herein was a "problem" for God. How could he be holy and deal with sin and yet at the same time be love and forgive the sinner?

The book of Romans shows how God solved his "dilemma." Romans 3:25 says, "Whom God hath set forth to be a propitiation through faith in his blood . . . . " We have a mercy seat. We have a satisfaction and it is the Lord Jesus Christ. When Jesus died on the cross of Calvary he absolutely satisfied the demands of God's law. At the same time he made it possible for God to forgive us. That is how much God loves us. He was willing to send Jesus to be the satisfaction for our sins.

C. The Savior

"We have seen and do testify that the Father sent the Son to be the Savior of the world" (1 John 4:14). Jesus came into the world to save us. Oh, what Jesus endured to be the Savior of the world. Oh, how they treated Jesus. They put nails in his hands, drove a spike into his ankles, thrust a spear in his side.

Mary, the human mother of Jesus, had a sword piercing through her heart; the cross broke her heart.

Think what God the Father went through when his Son was made sin for the whole human race. We do not have a segregated gospel. We do not have a gospel for one segment of this world. We have a gospel for all persons regardless of face, place, and race. Jesus, the universal Savior, says to a lost world, "I love you; I died for you. Come, whosoever will, let him come."

III. LOVE PRACTICED

John now turns to the practical affairs of everyday life. Love must be practiced by God's children. We are to live a life of love one to another.

A. A Commandment

Three times in these verses we are told to "love one another." Do you ever have to do that at home? Do you parents ever have to say, "Brothers and sisters, love one another"? God has to do that too.

In John 13 Jesus knew he would soon be leaving his disciples. They were going to represent him on earth. The way they lived and conducted themselves toward one another would be decisive in confronting the world with his saving claims. In John 13:34–35 Jesus said, "A new commandment I give unto you, That ye love one another; as I have loved you, that ye also love one another. By this shall all men know that ye are my disciples, if ye have love one to another." I can imagine John looking over at Simon Peter and silently thinking, "You mean I have to love that loud-mouthed Simon Peter?" I can imagine Simon Peter sitting on the other end of the table looking over at John: "I have to love that dreamer, that visionary?"

Colossians 1:4 talks about our faith in the Lord Jesus Christ and the love we have "to all the saints." Let me be very practical. Let me come down to earth with these verses of scripture. It does not say that everybody will be lovable. Some people are more lovable than others. Some folks are hard to love. But this is how people will be convinced that Christianity is real. If we can come together with different personalities, with our failures, faults, and all of that, and if we can respond to one another in an attitude of love, this world will be convinced that our faith is real. The world is never going to be convinced that Christianity amounts to a hill of beans if Christians do not love one another. "If we love one another," we know that "God dwelleth in us, and his love is perfected in us" (1 John 4:12).

At the beginning of verse 12 John says, "No man hath seen God at any time." That verse appears to be out of context. He says, "Nobody has ever seen God," and then he goes right on talking about love. How does that tie in?

Well, God is invisible, but people are able to see the invisible God at work in the lives of human beings who show love toward one another. When they see you and me loving one another, they get a vision of what God is like. When we love one another, "God's love is perfected." God's love reaches its goal in your life. God's love achieves its purpose.

Start trying it. Go out tomorrow and say, "Okay, I am going to love everybody I see today. I don't care how mean they are, I don't care how obnoxiously they treat me, I am going to love everybody." You will probably have a fuss with your wife before you leave the house! You are going to make a shattering, sobering discovery—that the harder you try to love others, the more impossible it will become. How are you going to do it then?

Anybody who does not believe the Bible is the word of God, and I mean word by word, just has not studied it. I am constantly amazed at how God puts the words together just exactly as they ought to be, word for word. Look at verse 13. "Hereby know we that we dwell in him, and he in us, because he hath given us of his Spirit." God did give us his Spirit, but that is not what this verse teaches. This verse teaches that he will give you *out of* his Spirit. You do not have that kind of love within you. Reach down into your well and you will come up dry. Reach down into your heart and there is no love there for one another. All right, God says then, "I will give you of my Spirit." Romans 5:5 says, "The love of God is shed abroad in our hearts by the Holy Ghost which is given unto us." You must have God's love flowing into your heart to help you to love one another. It is a commandment.

B. A Communion

Loving one another is also a communion. This word *dwelleth* (1 John 4:16) now pops up again. In chapter 2 it was translated "abide," and that word now speaks of our reciprocal communion with God. God lives in us, we live in God, and therefore we are in the atmosphere of love.

I had a man in my church who was the sweetest smelling man I ever met. I began to wonder, "What is he using?" Oh, he smelled lovely. Finally my curiosity got the best of my tact and I asked him. I said, "Why do you smell so good? You smell like a rose all of the time." He laughed and said, "Well, preacher, that is exactly right. I really do. I work for a wholesale florist. I am working with flowers all the time and I am around them so much I smell like them." Right there I learned something. Your atmosphere has a great deal to do with what you are. The closer you get to the God of love, the more you live in the atmosphere of the love of God, the more the fragrance of love will be evident to those around you. We need to ask God to fill us with his Spirit of love.

A missionary to the Navajo Indians came upon a very ill Navajo woman who had been deserted by her tribe. When she got sick, her tribe threw her out and left her in the brush to die. The missionaries found her, took her in, and a kind, compassionate Christian doctor nursed her back to physical health. When she heard what they had done, she could not understand it. "When my own people threw me out, why did you take me in?" They told her it was because of Jesus, because of the love of Jesus. By and by she was ready to receive Christ. They asked the missionary preacher to come. As the missionary preacher counseled with her in the hospital room, the others prayed that God would open her eyes to see clearly the gospel of Jesus Christ. About that time the door opened and in walked the missionary doctor. She looked over at him and said, "If this Jesus you are talking about is anything like *him*, I can trust him forever." We are so to live and so to demonstrate the love of Jesus Christ that it will be easy for those around us to trust him forever.

16

Perfect Love
1 John 4:17–21

I. Our Future
  A. Anxiety
  B. Assurance
II. Our Father
  A. Originated by the Father
  B. Reciprocated by the Family
III. Our Fellowman
  A. A Contradiction
  B. A Commandment

WHEN WE DEAL WITH THE SUBJECT OF GOD'S LOVE WE ARE TOUCHING ON a topic that is unfathomable. We can never plumb its depths.

Could we with ink the ocean fill
And were the skies of parchment made;
Were every stalk on earth a quill
And every man a scribe by trade;
To write the love of God above
Would drain the ocean dry;
Nor could the scroll contain the whole
Though stretched from sky to sky.

Were I to continue week by week, year by year, for the rest of my life, to preach on the subject of the love of God I could never fully tell it all.

In 1 John 4:17–21 the word *love* appears eleven times. The emphasis is on perfect love, love that has reached maturity, love that is complete. I want to make a correction in the text in verse 17. The better manuscripts translate verse 17, "Herein is love with us made perfect." This chapter has an interesting progression concerning love. Verse 12 says in the second sentence, "If we love one another, God dwelleth in us, and his love is perfected in us." There we see love's power in the life. In verse 16 we read, "And we have known and believed the love that God hath to us." That is love proven in the demonstration of the sacrifice of Jesus on Calvary. In verse 17 it says that love is perfected or completed with us. Here love is pictured as a companion walking hand in hand with a child of God as he or she moves toward the future and the day of judgment when we shall stand before God.

The Bible does not talk about our love as something that can be generated in our heart; rather, it talks about the perfect love exemplified in the Lord Jesus Christ. If I want to know about perfect love, I do not look within my heart. I do not find perfect love there. I have to look up to him to discover what perfect love is all about. Only as I let Jesus live in my heart and let the love of God flow unhindered in my life can my love grow and mature as God intends.

I. Our Future

Verses 17 and 18 cast our thoughts into the days of the future. Verse 17 talks about the day of judgment. Matthew 11:22 says, "It shall be more tolerable for Tyre and Sidon at the day of judgment, than for you." Matthew 12:36 says, "Every idle word that men shall speak, they shall give account thereof in the day of judgment. Paul teaches that God has "appointed a day, in the which he will judge the world in righteousness by that man whom he hath ordained" (Acts 17:31). Hebrews 9:27 says, "It is appointed unto men once to die, but after this the judgment."

A. Anxiety

People approach their meeting with God with one of two attitudes. In 1 John 4:18 we are told there may be anxiety about the
future. The word *fear* is used four times. "There is no fear in
love; but perfect love casteth out fear: because fear hath torment. He that feareth is not made perfect in love." This fear is
real. All kinds of phobias, all kinds of fears and trouble, perplex
and attack people's souls and minds—fear of exposure, fear of
death, fear of discovery, fear of the unknown, fear of other people, fear of the problems and the unexplainable things that will
come in life, fear on every side. But perhaps the worst kind of
fear we can experience is the fear of God. Multitudes of people
are afraid to think of him, afraid to meet him in judgment. They
do not want to entertain thoughts of God, yet they are afraid
that ultimately they must.

We know where fear was born. Genesis 3:10 says that fear was
born in the garden of Eden. When man sinned and disobeyed
God, Adam hid from God. When God confronted him, Adam
said, "I heard thy voice . . . and I was afraid." Fear came when
sin entered this world.

Fear has its own kind of torment or dread or punishment. Out
there in the future there is torment for the soul that rejects God.
Matthew 25:46 says, "And these shall go away into everlasting
punishment." The rich man in hell is pictured as saying, "Father Abraham, have mercy on me . . . I am tormented in this
flame" (Luke 16:24).

But torment can begin before eternity. The fear of judgment,
the fear of meeting God unprepared, the fear of not being ready
to meet him—sometimes that dread is the worst thing.

B. Assurance

"Perfect love casteth out fear" (1 John 4:18). For the lost person there is fear, but when one comes to Jesus Christ the love of
God moves into that heart. As the love of God develops in that
person's life it dispels fear. It is possible, according to these
verses, to face the future with assurance. "Herein is our love
made perfect, that we may have boldness in the day of judgment." "Boldness" means confidence or openness of heart, no

sense of shame. It is possible for the child of God to look forward to meeting God with complete assurance in his or her heart.

How is this possible? The last part of verse 17 says to us, "As he is [talking about Jesus], so are we in this world." This is one reason we can face the future with assurance in our heart.

To be as he is means at least two things. First, it has to do with our representation of him. A translation could be, "As he is in heaven representing us, so we are in this world representing him." That is the way it ought to be. Jesus is representing us in heaven as our intercessor, our spokesman at the right hand of God. He represents us up there and we represent him down here. If we represent him adequately, reflecting his love, then when we stand before him we need not fear. We have perfect confidence.

Second, to be as he is also means identification. That is, as he (Jesus) is in relation to judgment, so are we in this world. As Jesus Christ has already experienced the judgment, we have the same relationship to judgment that Jesus Christ now has. One of the sweetest truths in all the Bible is the teaching that the child of God will not have to meet judgment because that judgment has already been borne by the Lord Jesus. In John 5:24 Jesus said, "He that heareth my word, and believeth on him that sent me, hath everlasting life, and shall not come into condemnation; but is passed from death unto life." Jesus' statement simply means that he has already borne our judgment. Our sins were laid on him and in his death on Calvary God put our sins to death. God judged our sins once and for all. Romans 8:1 says, "There is therefore now no condemnation to them which are in Christ Jesus." If we are in Christ, if we are located in him by the new birth, we do not have to shake with fear as we think about the days of the future and the judgment of God.

Suppose you visit a court tomorrow. You walk in there, sit down, and watch the proceedings without any anxiety in your heart. You are there with that sense of assurance because you know that nothing is coming up against you. No judgment is due you.

John says in verse 18, "He that feareth is not made perfect in love." That is, if a child of God does have fear in his heart, if a child of God still has anxiety as he looks toward the future, it means that the love of God is not perfected or completed in his heart.

Two young people are studying for an algebra test. One of them studies well. He learns all the formulas. He goes over all of the problems. The other one, on the other hand, does not study much. He spends a lot of time going other places. He plays ball all afternoon. He does not master the formulas. He does not go over earlier exams and quizzes or review the problems given in the book. So one student looks forward to the algebra test with assurance. The other one looks forward to it fearfully. So it is with you and me. If we have not lived for Jesus Christ, if our life is not characterized by love, then we are not made perfect in love and therefore we fear.

II. Our Father

"We love [the word *him* is not in the better manuscripts], because he first loved us" (1 John 4:19).

A. Originated by the Father

Love originates with the Father. Love has its fountainhead, source, origin, in God the Father. Love does not begin in the heart of man. The heart of man is filled with hate, hostility, prejudice. The heart of man is filled with evil and murder. Men hate one another; men hate God. But "God is love," scripture says, and the love of God flowed into this world in the person of the Lord Jesus Christ. You and I do not have to do one thing to get God to love us. We do not have to cause God somehow to love us. The Bible says that he has loved us with an everlasting love.

Before the stars were put in place, before the earth was molded together, before the universe was created, God loved us with an everlasting love. God loved you *first*. Jesus Christ did not die to cause God to love us. Rather, because God did love us he sent his Son Jesus to die. Scripture says, "But God commendeth [that is, God proves, God exhibits, God shows] his love toward us, in that, while we were yet sinners, Christ died for us" (Romans 5:8). Because God first loved, he sent his Son. Love is originated by the Father.

B. Reciprocated by the Family

"He first loved; we love." Something about the love of God calls for a response in our heart. When we understand the love of God, when it dawns on us that God really loves us, it is easy to love in return.

III. OUR FELLOWMAN

In 1 John 4:20–21 we see perfect love as it relates to our fellowman. These verses become very practical and searching in their thrust to our heart.

A. A Contradiction

John begins this section by saying, "If a man say . . . ," the seventh time that particular formula is used. John is talking about people making a profession that they love God. But, you see, profession does not prove possession.

John gives us a startling contradiction. "If a man say, I love God, and hateth his brother, he is a liar" (1 John 4:20). When we read the writings of John we discover something about him. He never saw things in gray. As far as John was concerned, things were either black or white, no shades in between.

In Psalm 116:1 the psalmist says, "I love the Lord, because he hath heard my voice and my supplications." It is fine to say you love God, but John is saying, "You have to go a step farther." It is not enough to say, "I love God." You have to be truthful in that statement, and one of the ways to tell if you are truthful is to examine yourself concerning your relationship to your brother. Do you love your brother? People who profess to love God yet at the same time have ugliness and coldness and hatred and prejudice in their heart toward their brother have conceived in their own mind an imaginary God who will allow them to love him while at the same time to hate their fellowman. Theirs is not the God of the Bible, not the God of love. John presents it so clearly we just cannot miss it.

Peter puts it this way: "Whom having not seen, ye love" (1 Peter 1:8). John is saying, "How in the world can you claim to love the invisible when you don't love the visible? How can you claim to love God and not love his creation?"

I want to emphasize with all of the conviction of my soul that the modern church is going to have to come to grips with the contradiction of a position that makes it possible for them to say, "I love God," yet at the same time to have prejudice in their heart toward any other human being regardless of that person's place or race. There is an inherent contradiction in the position of a church that will say, "I love God," but will close its doors to someone who needs to hear the gospel.

The gospel of the Lord Jesus Christ is a gospel of love, and one of its premises is: "Whosoever will, let him come." I would not preach if I could not stand and preach a "whosoever will" gospel. This gospel is for the whole world, and the love of God demands that I love my fellowman. Now I did not say I have to love that person's ways. I don't love everybody's ways, do you? In fact, I don't even love all of my own ways (though I love me pretty good!). So, we have to love others, even when we disagree with what they're doing.

B. A Commandment

Here is God's commandment: "He who loveth God love his brother also" (1 John 4:21). When we violate the commandment of God and do not obey him, God will judge us for our disobedience.

Dr. Stephen Olford told the story of how they prayed through this matter of an open-door policy in their church saying, "Whosoever will, let him come." They prayed through the matter; they did not do it hastily. They allowed the Holy Spirit time to move in people's hearts and let love grow and mature and perfect itself. This business of loving people is not something that can be legislated. You cannot make people love one another. You do not put people in the same building and say, "All right, love one another." But through much prayer and soul-searching and the leadership of the Holy Spirit they arrived at an open-door policy in their church. Seven men strongly opposed that position and voted against it in the church. Within a year's time all seven of those men had died and six of them had an untimely death. You do not violate the word of God and live in open disobedience without incurring the wrath of God on your life and on your church. The blessings of God will never fall as they ought to fall on a congregation that lives in the moral contradiction of saying, "I love God but I do not love my fellowman."

Two city churches just two blocks apart had a bus ministry. The first of these churches picked up children of another race and when they were brought to the church some people in that church created a turmoil. They demonstrated an absolutely un-Christian attitude about the matter and were vehement in their expressions of disgust. The people got together and decided, "We are not going to allow those children to come into our church." Within a matter of months that church was involved in such turmoil and upheaval that it began to go downhill. The last time I heard, it was in danger of bankruptcy.

The other church with a bus ministry prayed through this matter. They said, "We have to recognize that if you love God, you have to love your fellowman regardless of who he is." They adopted the policy, "Whosoever will, let him come." And not too many weeks ago they baptized the first person of another race in that church. There may have been one or two backslidden Christians who did not know much about the love of God who complained about it. But clearly the blessings of God have been on that church in a remarkable way.

I am a southerner. I have had to come to grips in my own heart with prejudices and animosities that have been in me by virtue of my heritage. But if you are truly a born-again Christian and the love of God is coming to perfection in your life, and if you will be honest and open about it and will pray and let the love of God grow and develop in your life, God will help you conquer your prejudices. Don't ever allow where people come from or the color of their skin or how they are dressed or how they look keep you from loving them and telling them about Jesus. John says, "If you say you love God whom you have not seen, how can you not love your brother whom you have seen?" Let's take that teaching to heart and show some love to our brothers and sisters!

17

Birthmarks of a Believer

1 John 5:1–5

I. APPRECIATION OF GOD'S CHILDREN
  A. God's Children Love the Father
  B. God's Children Love the Family
II. APPLICATION OF GOD'S COMMANDMENTS
  A. Desire
  B. Delight
III. APPROPRIATION OF GOD'S CONQUEST
  A. The Initial Conquest
  B. The Continual Conquest

THE BIBLE DESCRIBES WHAT IT MEANS TO KNOW JESUS CHRIST AS PERSONAL Savior in many ways. John, for example, talks about being born again or being born of God. John uses the expression, "born of God," seven times in this book. He emphasizes the truth that before anyone can get into heaven it is essential that he or she be born of God.

The Bible indicates that there are two kinds of birth. In Matthew 11:11 Jesus said of John the baptist, "Verily I say unto you, Among them that are born of women there hath not risen a greater than John the Baptist: notwithstanding he that is least in the kingdom of heaven is greater than he." The first way all of us are born is to be born of woman. All of us have experienced a physical birth.

Also, the Bible says, it is possible for a person to be born of God. This is what is meant by being born again. Nicodemus was a ruler of the Jews, a rabbi, a religious leader. He was a prominent and pious man, yet Jesus said to him, "Verily, verily, I say unto thee, Except a man be born again, he cannot see the kingdom of God" (John 3:3).

Nicodemus did not understand what Jesus was talking about. "How can a man be born when he is old? can he enter the second time into his mother's womb, and be born?" To which Jesus replied, "Verily, verily, I say unto thee, Except a man be born of water and of the Spirit, he cannot enter into the kingdom of God." Jesus told this religious man that he had to be born again. He had to be born of the Spirit; he had to have a second birth. This is the only way anyone can come into the family of God.

Not only is the new birth an essential experience, but it is also a definite experience. What would you say if I should come up to you and ask, "Have you ever been born physically?" Well, you would look at me as if I were crazy and reply, "Of course, I have been born physically. There is no question about it. I am living, I am growing, I am moving. You know very well that I have been born physically." Birth is a definite occurrence; it is something that you can know has happened.

The new birth, being born again, being born of the Spirit, is also a definite experience. Yet when you ask people, "Are you a Christian; have you been born again?" they may say, "Well, I think so," or "Well, maybe so," or "I hope so." The Bible declares that the new birth is something we can know has taken place in our life.

How does the new-birth experience come about? How is it possible for someone to know Christ as personal Savior? First John 5:1 says, "Whosoever believeth that Jesus is the Christ is born of God." When the Bible says that believing on Jesus Christ is essential to being born of God, what does it mean? Does it mean that I can believe intellectually that Jesus Christ came into the world, that he died on the cross for my sins? Is that what it means? Why, of course not. Multitudes of people believe that Jesus Christ lived, and even that he is the Savior of the world.

They have an intellectual belief in Jesus Christ, yet they are not born again.

John 1:12-13 says, "But as many as received him, to them gave he power to become the sons of God, even to them that believe on his name: Which were born, not of blood, nor of the will of the flesh, nor of the will of man, but of God." John says that to believe on the Lord Jesus Christ means to receive him into your heart as your personal Savior. This is the most important fact in life. The denomination you embrace is not of primary importance. The main issue is not whether you are a church member. The crucial issue of life is this: Have you been born again? Has Jesus Christ come into your life? Have you been born into the family of God?

The new birth is an experience that revolutionizes one's life. In 2 Corinthians 5:17 we read, "Therefore if any man be in Christ [that is, born again into the family of God], he is a new creature: old things are passed away; behold, all things are become new." Definite changes take place in a life that has been born into the family of God.

There are some ways you can recognize a born-again believer and know in your own heart whether or not you are truly a child of God.

Every family has certain definitive physical characteristics. You know that some people are in a particular family because of the size or curvature of their nose. You know that others are members of a particular family because of the size of their frame. Likewise, there are some birthmarks of the believer. These verses show us three birthmarks of a born-again child of God, three ways to know that you are a child of the king.

I. APPRECIATION OF GOD'S CHILDREN

John says, "Every one that loveth him that begat [that is, loveth the Father] loveth him also that is begotten of him [that is, every member of the family]" (1 John 5:1). Two things are stated in this verse of scripture.

A. God's Children Love the Father

A born-again person loves the heavenly Father, "him that begat." That is the normal thing. It is self-evident that a child will love his father. "We love him, because he first loved us" (1 John 4:19). The love of Jesus Christ flows into our heart and it responds to the overtures of the love of God. Galatians 4:6 says, "And because ye are sons, God hath sent forth the Spirit of his Son into your hearts, crying, Abba, Father." It is normal and natural for God's children to love the heavenly Father. The more we come to know about God, the more we understand what God has done for us, the easier it is for us to love him. The more I comprehend the sacrifice of Calvary, and the more I understand how much my heavenly Father sacrificed in order to send his Son Jesus into this world, the more I love Him.

B. God's Children Love the Family

When you were born physically you were born into a family with a mother, a father, and perhaps brothers and sisters. When you are born into God's family you also have brothers and sisters. It is a natural thing for family members to love one another. Psalm 68:6 says, "God setteth the solitary in families." This is one of the most precious things about being a Christian, to know that as a child of God I have other brothers and sisters in Jesus Christ.

As a born-again child of God I am a brother in the Lord of every other born-again child of God. It does not matter what their particular church may be. If they are born of the Father and I am born of the Father, they are my brother or sister in Jesus and I love them. It does not matter what color their skin may be. It does not matter what their particular upbringing or cultural standing is. If they know the heavenly Father, then I can be in fellowship with them. We love those who are members of our family.

How does love conduct itself toward those family members? First Corinthians 12:26 says, "And whether one member suffer, all the members suffer with it." There is an understanding, a concern, an interest, on the part of all of God's children for every member of the family.

First Corinthians 13:4 elaborates on the meaning of love. "Charity suffereth long, and is kind; charity envieth not; charity vaunteth not itself, is not puffed up." This is how love behaves toward members of the family of God. When you meet for the first time a person who knows Christ as Savior, is there love in your heart? One of the birthmarks of the believer is an appreciation of God's family.

I think of the story of Paul and Silas preaching the gospel in Philippi. They got put in jail for their testimony. The Philippian jailer scourged them and beat them until there were stripes and whelps on them. At midnight Paul and Silas were singing praises to God and praying. I wonder if God was enjoying the music so much that he started tapping his foot, which caused an earthquake, and the jail doors came flinging open! The jailer thought he had lost his prisoners, but they said, "Do thyself no harm: for we are all here" (Acts 16:28). You remember what happened. The jailer rushed in and said, "Sirs, what must I do to be saved?" And they said, "Believe on the Lord Jesus Christ, and thou shalt be saved, and thy house" (Acts 16:30–31). He did believe and receive Jesus Christ as his Lord and Savior, and that night at midnight he was born into the family of God.

Now watch the difference in his life. He took Paul and Silas, washed their stripes, put a meal on the table before them, and fellowshiped with them. He who "loveth him that begat loveth him also that is begotten of him." If you are truly born again, the birthmark of love will be characteristic of your life.

II. Application of God's Commandments

A second birthmark of those who are born again is the application of God's commandments. Twice in 1 John 5:2–3 we are told that the children of God love him and keep his commandments.

A. Desire

If we are truly a born-again child of God, we will desire to keep God's commandments. In the Old Testament the commandments of God were imposed on the children of Israel as a matter of strict duty. They were required to obey them. In the New Testament the Pharisees went to great extremes to keep the outward letter of the law. Religion to them was largely a matter of external duty or responsibility. When love comes into the picture, however, one's duty to obey the law is transformed into a desire to obey the law.

When you meet Christ and are born into the family of God, because you love him, you desire to obey him and do everything God wants you to do. When the Bible says, "Thou shalt not take the name of the Lord thy God in vain" (Exodus 20:7), that is no duty to you. It is the desire of your heart that you never take his name in vain. When the Bible says that you are to "remember the sabbath day, to keep it holy" (Exodus 20:8), that is no duty to you. The desire of your heart is that you might serve him faithfully on that day—and everyday. When you are born into God's family, the duty of the law becomes the deepest desire of your heart.

B. Delight

Keeping God's law also becomes the delight of your life. "His commandments are not grievous" (1 John 5:3). They are not burdensome, not heavy. It becomes a delight to do the will of God. In Matthew 23:3–4 Jesus talks about the Pharisees and their religion. "All therefore whatsoever they bid you observe, that observe and do; but do not ye after their works: for they say, and do not. For they bind heavy burdens and grievous to be borne, and lay them on men's shoulders." They made religion a burden. To obey the laws they imposed was a grievous experience, but Jesus Christ came into the world and taught us that through the new birth we can delight in the law of God. When people's experience of religion is burdensome, it is because they misunderstand the commandments of God. God does not give his commandments to make our life miserable and to restrain us from joyful things. The commandments of God are given because of his love, concern, and interest in every one of us.

Think about a little boy whose father says to him, "Do not touch the stove. The stove is hot." If the little boy puts his hand on the stove he is going to be burned. So the father issues a command. "Thou shalt not touch the stove." What motivates the father to give such a directive? Is it the desire to make life miserable for the son? Of course not. The desire of the father is to protect his child from injury. The commandment is imposed out of love. When we understand that the commandments of God are the reflection of God's care for us, the greatest delight of our life becomes to keep them.

Scripture says in Psalm 37:5, "Commit thy way unto the Lord; trust also in him; and he shall bring it to pass." What a pleasure it becomes to serve the Lord Jesus Christ! And here is a wonderful thing—when Christians start living for Christ, when they start doing the will of God in the power of the indwelling Holy Spirit, they make two remarkable discoveries. They discover first of all that in doing the will of God, they find great liberty and freedom.

The world clamors for liberty. Everywhere you turn people are saying, "I want to be free. I want to live without restrictions. I want freedom, give me freedom, give me liberty." Yet in their pursuit of liberty and freedom, in their desire to do what they want to do regardless of God's law, they do not find freedom. Rather, they find bondage and slavery and shame. On the other hand, when a person says, "I will do thy will, O God," scripture says, "In the keeping of them [God's laws] there is great reward" (Psalm 19:11). The obedient one finds release, freedom, fulfillment. We find everything we were looking for when we willingly submit to the will of God.

Not only do we find freedom but we find joy in keeping the commandments of God. If we love God, the Bible says we will want to keep his commandments, and then when we keep his commandments we discover a remarkable thing. It makes us happy. I think of what scripture says in Psalm 119:54, "Thy statutes have been my songs in the house of my pilgrimage." Can you imagine putting the local traffic code to music? Can you imagine singing the local blue laws? Yet this is what Christians discover. In keeping the law of God there flows a joy through life we have never experienced before.

III. Appropriation of God's Conquest

Birthmark number three is the appropriation of God's conquest. "For whatsoever is born of God overcometh the world" (1 John 5:4). Three times John uses the word *overcometh*, which lets us know that a real conflict is going on in the world. It never makes the newspaper, it is never shown on television, but a life-

and-death struggle is going on in this world: the conflict between the born-again child of God and the hosts of hell. The
Bible says that Christians fight against three formidable foes:
the world, the flesh, and the devil. Further, the Bible declares
that Christians can experience overcoming, conquest, and
victory.

There is no reason at all to be a defeated Christian. If you are a
born-again child of God, everything you need for victory is
available to you. Two different tenses of the verb *overcometh*
are used. The first and third time it is used in the present tense;
it is a daily overcoming. The second time it is used in a tense
that means something took place in the past and was settled
once and for all. This is the victory that overcame the world; it
took place in the past.

A. The Initial Conquest

Human beings are not able to conquer this world. You and I
are not strong enough to conquer it. Within our own abilities
and capabilities, we are not a match for this world. In ourselves we are powerless to overcome the world. Adam and
Eve learned this to their sorrow. They met the temptations,
the lust of the flesh and the lust of the eyes and the pride of
life, in their own strength. Rather than conquering, they
were the conquered. They were the vanquished. Someone
had to come into the world, meet it on its own ground, and
win absolute, total victory.

Some two thousand years ago Jesus Christ came into the
world, " . . . and the world was made by him, and the world
knew him not" (John 1:10). What a paradox. Here was the one
who created the world, yet when he came, the world did not
recognize him. It was hostile to him; it battled against him. The
world did everything it could to conquer the Lord Jesus Christ.
Every possible temptation was hurled at him, yet at the climax
of his ministry the Lord Jesus said in John 16:33, "In the world
ye shall have tribulation: but be of good cheer; I have overcome
the world." Christ has gotten us the victory.

So this world gathered its forces. It moved in heavy artillery
and began to blast the Lord Jesus Christ. Finally, the world put
him on a cross and unleashed its mightiest weapon, the power

of death. But when the dust cleared and the light dawned, there was an empty tomb. The Lord Jesus Christ, with the keys of death, hell, and grave, ascended to the Father, leading captivity captive. He is the captain of our salvation; he is the conquering Christ. In the work of Jesus Christ, going from the cross through the tomb back to the right hand of the Father, we have all that is necessary for total victory.

B. The Continual Conquest

Because Jesus Christ overcame, we can overcome. In the present tense these words speak of continual conquest. Because Jesus Christ conquered we may appropriate the Christ-life into our daily life. The potential for daily victory over every temptation and obstacle this world has to place in your course is yours. Romans 8:37 says that we are (and Paul makes up a word) "superconquerors" through him that loved us.

In 2 Corinthians 2:14 Paul may have been envisioning those days when the Roman generals came back to the city of Rome, having won victory on a foreign field. The victorious parade was assembled and the vanquished captives were tied in chains behind the army. The incense of victory was in the air and Paul imagined Christ the conquering general marching, leading that triumphal train. "Now thanks be unto God, which always causeth us to triumph in Christ." This is victory in Jesus. First Corinthians 15:57 exclaims, "But thanks be to God, which giveth us the victory through our Lord Jesus Christ."

Perhaps you say to me, "I am a born-again believer and I am defeated. I am a child of God and yet I live a life of daily defeat in my Christian experience. How do you get this victory you're talking about?" What does the Bible say? "This is the victory that overcometh the world, even our fighting?" Is that what John says? No, that is not what he says. "This is the victory that overcometh the world, even our faith" (1 John 5:4). Faith is the switch that turns on the power of Christ into our life.

In Hebrews 11 we read about the great men and women of God and their accomplishments. We read about Enoch and Noah and Abraham and Sara and Moses and Rahab and all of those great heroes in the Old Testament. How did they do it? Without exception it says about every one of them, "By faith, by faith." By faith we claim what Jesus Christ has for us and we are thereby able to overcome this world. It is there for us. The victory is ours if we are children of God.

After the Civil War a poor man, a beggar, wandered from place to place with very little subsistence. Everywhere he went he bragged about the fact that he had Abraham Lincoln's name on a piece of paper. He did not have anything else, he was about to starve to death, but he said, "I have Abraham Lincoln's name on a piece of paper." Another fellow said, "I don't believe that." The poor man said, "I certainly do; I'll prove it to you." He reached into a grimy pocket and pulled out a worn and dirty piece of paper. The other man unfolded it and said, "Do you realize what you have here? You certainly do have Abraham Lincoln's name on a piece of paper. Abraham Lincoln has given you a very generous pension. Abraham Lincoln has made you rich and you are living like a pauper. All you have to do is redeem that claim and you will be rich!" I want to say to you Christians, Jesus Christ has made you rich; claim it by faith. "This is the victory that overcometh the world."

Someone says to me, "Preacher, I would like to be a Christian but I cannot live the life." Of course, you cannot live it. If you are going to wait around until you think you can live the life, you will die in your sins and you will never know the joy of being a Christian. You do not have the power, you do not have the equipment, you do not have the resources within your own fallen, depraved nature to live one day, one hour, one second, for the Lord Jesus Christ. But the good news of the gospel is that Jesus Christ through the new-birth experience will give you a new nature, the nature of God, the indwelling Holy Spirit, and Jesus Christ can meet the battles for you and conquer them, giving you victory.

There was a schoolboy, just a little kid, who was constantly antagonized by a big bully. Have you ever had that happen to you? When you were in school, did you ever have a big bully run you home every day? This little boy's life was miserable. Every day he would get out of school and here would come that big bully. One day he saw the bully. He took off for home! As he ran he looked ahead and there was his big brother, a senior in high school. He wheeled around behind his brother, got hold of his knees, stuck his head out between his big brother's legs, and said, "All right, now, come on, come on!" What a picture: Little brother, big bully, big brother. We come to the Lord Jesus Christ, our big brother, hide ourself in him, appropriate his conquest, and we can say to the world, "Come on, come on!"

18

The Witness of the Spirit
1 John 5:6–13

I. To the Son
   A. His Coming
   B. His Cleansing
II. In the Saint
   A. To Us, Facts
   B. With Us, Faith
   C. In Us, Feelings
III. Through the Scriptures
   A. The Source of Eternal Life
   B. The Substance of Eternal Life
   C. The Surety of Eternal Life

THE BIBLE TEACHES THAT THE CHRISTIAN HAS A "KNOW-SO" SALVATION. IN the book of 1 John the word *know* is used almost forty times. We can know beyond the shadow of a doubt that we are a child of God. First John 5:13 could well be called the key verse of this epistle.

The Bible tells us that it is possible for Christians to have certainty in life, that we can live in confidence that we each are genuinely and truly a child of God.

We are living in an age of uncertainty. Many things are no longer certain. We cannot be sure about some things we used to feel secure about. We are in a time of doubt and unbelief.

In these verses the Lord wants to give us divine authentication of the fact that we can know we are a child of God. A word that occurs many times in 1 John 5:6–13 is the word *witness*. At times in the King James version it is translated "witness." At other times it is translated "record," and on occasion it is translated "testimony" or "testify." This word occurs ten times in these verses. John is referring to the witness of the Holy Spirit of God, that divine authentication given by God to his children to let them know they indeed are his.

Three simple aspects of the witness of the Holy Spirit are important to keep in mind.

I. To the Son

First, the Holy Spirit of God bears witness to the Son of God, the Lord Jesus Christ (1 John 5:6–8). Every time the Holy Spirit is prominent in the Bible he is doing his main work of exalting the Lord Jesus. "Howbeit when he, the Spirit of truth, is come, he will guide you into all truth" (John 16:13). He will not speak about himself, but will bear witness to the Lord.

The Holy Spirit of God delights to exalt the Lord Jesus Christ. From beginning to end, the Spirit who inspired the pages of the Bible magnifies the Lord Jesus. So we know that the Lord Jesus Christ is truly the Son of God because of the witness of the Holy Spirit.

"Because the Spirit is truth" (1 John 6:6), whatever the Holy Spirit says is true. The Holy Spirit cannot lie; he cannot bear witness to what is not true. John is saying that everything the Bible says about Jesus Christ is absolutely certain, absolutely true.

The Holy Spirit bears witness to the Son in a twofold manner.

A. His Coming

The Spirit witnesses to the factuality of the Son's coming into the world. "This is he that came by water and blood, even Jesus Christ" (1 John 5:6).

As has been noted earlier, a particular heresy lies in the background for this book. A group of people, the Cerinthians, believed that Jesus was a mere man. At his baptism, however, the eternal Christ came upon him, abode upon him until the cross, and then was withdrawn, so that Jesus died as a mere man. One purpose of John's writing his gospel and epistles was to refute such ideas.

We are told that Jesus "came by water and blood," an allusion to the beginning and the climax of our Lord's ministry. The Lord Jesus Christ inaugurated his public ministry by a public baptism. He did it, not because he was a sinner and needed to identify himself with the repentance preached by John the baptist, but in order "to fulfill all righteousness."

When Jesus was baptized in water, the heavens opened up and all three persons of the godhead converged. God the Son came out of the water; God the Holy Spirit descended on him like a dove; and God the Father spoke from heaven and said, "This is my beloved Son, in whom I am well pleased" (Matthew 3:17).

Scripture also says that he came by blood. John is saying that Jesus was just as much the Christ in the moment he died on that cross as he was at his baptism experience. He did not cease to be Christ. He did not cease to be the eternal Son of God. God was intimately involved in the death that took place at the cross of Calvary. Jesus was God in human flesh dying for you and for me.

In 1 Timothy 1:15 the Bible says, "This is a faithful saying, and worthy of all acceptation, that Christ Jesus came into the world to save sinners; of whom I am chief." This is the reason he came: to put away sin by the sacrifice of himself. He came to make it possible for human beings to be reconciled to God. Every time the gospel is preached, every time this story of the coming of Jesus Christ is proclaimed, the Holy Spirit of God is at work in that situation bearing witness to the factuality of his coming.

B. His Cleansing

John also had a deeper, more spiritual meaning. He is also bearing witness to the cleansing of Jesus Christ in the shedding of his blood and the water at the cross. John often has a deeper meaning in his words, a beneath-the-surface meaning. For example, in John 19:34 we are told about the cross of Jesus.

Jesus Christ now is already dead. When the soldiers came to

break his legs, they did not break them, because he was already dead (John 19:6). Then in his hatred a soldier with a spear came to Jesus and with the spear he "pierced his side, and forthwith came there out blood and water" (John 19:34). Because of this statement some physicians believe that Jesus Christ died of a broken heart. Around the heart there is a sac of fluid and sometimes when the heart bursts, this sac of fluid also bursts. Jesus Christ had the weight of the sins of the world on him when he went to the cross and I think it broke his heart. The words *blood* and *water* are a testimony of his twofold cleansing power.

Jesus came by blood. When Jesus died on the cross he died a death where blood was shed, and the blood testifies to our judicial cleansing. The blood testifies to the fact that when God looks at a sinner who has received Christ as Savior he looks at a sinner who has been washed in the precious blood of the lamb. "The blood of Jesus Christ his Son cleanseth us from all sin" (1 John 1:7). In the cross of Jesus, my sins have been fully dealt with. I have been cleansed from the penalty of sin. Never a sin will be brought up against you or held against your account before God, because your sins have been washed away in the blood of the lamb.

Jesus came by water, and this has to do with our practical or daily cleansing. When you walked into the Old Testament tabernacle, there was first of all a brazen altar where the sacrifice was made and second there was a laver, a big basin of water. That pictures the normal progression of our experience with God. First we have to come to the altar where the sacrifice is made, where the blood of the lamb is poured out. Then we must also go to the laver of water where we experience daily cleansing from the practice and power of sin in our life. God has made it possible for us not only to be saved from sin's penalty, but we can be saved from sin's power on a day-to-day basis.

Salvation does not leave us in the shackles of daily bondage. God has made it possible for us to have daily victory over the power of sin in our life. Ephesians 5:26 says, "That he might sanctify and cleanse it [his church] with the washing of water by the word." The hymn writer puts it this way:

> Let the water and the blood
> From thy wounded side which flowed,

Be of sin the double cure,
Save from wrath and make me pure.

II. In the Saint

Second, the Holy Spirit also witnesses in the saint. "If we receive the witness of men, the witness of God is greater" (1 John 5:9). That word *if* means "since." There is no question about it. John is not raising a question about whether or not we receive the witness of men. We live on a daily basis of receiving the testimony of men. We take people's word every day.

Someone said to me, "I would like to believe in the Lord but I just cannot have faith." The Bible says in Romans 12:3 that "God hath dealt to every man the measure of faith." God has given you a natural capacity for faith.

Don't talk to me about your atheism. No one is born an atheist. You were born with a nature that would cause you to believe there is a God. Your nature has fallen, true, yet it has not fallen so far that it cannot believe there is a God. If you are living in unbelief, you have taught yourself to disbelieve.

Jesus never said, "You cannot come to me that you may have life." Jesus says, "Ye will not come to me, that you may have life."

We live by faith every day of our life. It would be a terrible experience to try to live one day without receiving the witness of men. Can you imagine how a day without that kind of faith would be?

You would wake up in the morning and say, "Oh my, I am afraid to go downstairs. I bet my wife has put strychnine in the food. If I eat those pancakes I am going to be poisoned."

Then you say, "My, I am afraid to use that toothpaste. I am afraid some evil person has put cyanide in the toothpaste and if I use it, it will kill me."

You get in your car and say, "Oh, I am scared to start the engine. What if it's wired to a bomb?"

So you walk rather than drive to the office building where you work and you say, "Oh, gracious, I am afraid to get in the elevator. What if its cables should break?"

So you trudge up eight flights of stairs and the doctor calls. "We have the report from your recent examination."

You think, "How do I know I can trust those lab tests?"

Nonetheless, you go by the drugstore to pick up your prescription and you say to yourself, "Well, I don't know whether to take this medicine or not. I don't know if I have enough faith in the druggist. What if the pharmacist gave me the wrong pills?"

You see, life would be impossible if we were unwilling to receive the "witness of men." John is saying, "You receive the witness of men, you accept the testimony of men," but "the witness of God is greater."

God bears witness to his children about salvation. He witnesses in the saint in three ways.

A. To Us, Facts

In Hebrews 10:15 the word of God says, "The Holy Ghost also is a witness to us. The Holy Spirit witnesses to the Christian about the facts of the gospel. Every time the word of God is proclaimed, every time the true gospel is delivered, the Spirit of God lets us know we are hearing the truth. Suppose someone is an unbeliever, not interested in knowing Christ as Savior. Yet as the word of God is declared in the power of the Spirit, the Spirit lets that person know down deep inside his or her heart that what is being preached is true: "That man is telling the truth." "That is real." "That is right."

B. With Us, Faith

More is said about the person of the Holy Spirit in Romans 8 than in any place in the word of God. So in Romans 8:16 the Bible says, "The Spirit itself . . ." The Holy Spirit of God is a divine person, not an impersonal force or power. "The Spirit itself beareth witness with our spirit." Do you see the progression? The Holy Spirit presents you with the gospel, gives you an opportunity to hear the objective facts of the gospel, and so down in your heart is the desire to be saved. Down in your heart is the desire to reach out by faith and take those facts about Jesus Christ and bring them into your heart. When you have that desire, the Holy Spirit lets you know that your faith is genuine. He bears "witness to us"; that is the fact of the gospel. He bears "witness with us"; that is the faith of the gospel.

C. In Us, Feelings

In 1 John 5:10 we read, "He that believeth on the Son of God hath the witness in himself." That is where feeling comes in. Most people have it reversed. People who are lost have the idea that they can be saved only when they feel like being saved. They say, "You know I was in a church one time and I really felt moved. I didn't do anything about it, and I don't feel like that now, but if I ever feel like that again, then . . . ."

God is under no obligation to give you any kind of feelings you want to have in order to be saved. If you can determine the kind of feelings you must have to be saved, in essence you are setting up the terms of salvation. The way God puts it is not feelings, faith, and then facts. No, God's order is facts, faith, and then feelings. You are not saved because you feel good. You are not saved because you feel saved. You must come to God God's way. You have to come to God on his basis.

I once asked a man, "How do you know you are saved?" And he answered, "Oh, I know because, man, when I got saved I did backflips and I felt whoopty-doopties in my heart and I got this tingling feeling all over." I am not making fun of that, but you are not saved because you feel good. If you know you are saved, however, you can certainly feel good about that.

Believing is the root and *feeling* is the fruit, and we must always keep them in the proper order. I have more feeling about my salvation now than I did when I was saved as a nine-year-old. Then I did not understand what had happened to me. All I knew was that I was a little boy lost and Jesus died on the cross for me. I knew if I would ask him to forgive me, he would, and he would come into my heart and life and be my Savior. So I asked him and he came in and he saved me. Since that time, as I have read and studied the word of God for myself, I have run across wonderful things I never dreamed of when I received Christ as my Savior. The Holy Spirit bears witness to the Son; that is the historical witness. He bears witness in the saint; that is the experiential witness.

III. THROUGH THE SCRIPTURES

Third, the Holy Spirit bears witness through the scriptures. "These things have I written to you that believe . . . that ye may know . . . " (1 John 5:13).

Do you believe that George Washington ever lived? How do you know he lived? Have you ever seen him? Have you heard his voice? Why do you believe George Washington lived? You read it in a book.

God has let us know that salvation is certain and secure by putting it down in a book. Psalm 119:89 says, "For ever, O Lord, thy word is settled in heaven." God put it down in a book.

A. The Source of Eternal Life

"This is the record, that God hath given to us eternal life, and this life is in his Son" (1 John 5:11). Apart from Jesus there is no life.

Jesus Christ is the source of physical life. John says, "All things were made by him; and without him was not any thing made that was made" (John 1:3). The Bible says that Christ is upholding all things by the word of his power.

All spiritual life comes from the Lord Jesus. "I am come that they might have life, and that they might have it more abundantly" (John 10:10). Jesus Christ not only opens the door; he says, "I am the door." Jesus Christ not only promises bread, he says, "I am the bread." Jesus Christ not only shows the way; he says, "I am the way." Jesus Christ not only bestows life; he says, "I am the way, the truth, and the life" (John 14:6). He is the source of life.

B. The Substance of Eternal Life

"He that hath the Son hath life" (1 John 5:12). If you have Jesus, you have life. Suppose I take this Bible and put a pen inside it. Then I say to you, "I am going to give you this book." When I give you this book, you also get the pen. That is what John is telling us here. "He that hath the Son hath life." When you get the book, Jesus, you get the pen, life. When you receive

Christ you receive eternal life. If you do not have Jesus, then you do not have life.

A young man was thinking about receiving Jesus as his personal Savior and said, "I am not sure I can pay the price of what it takes to become a Christian." The man who was witnessing to him said, "Have you ever considered what it costs not to become a Christian?"

C. The Surety of Eternal Life

The Son is the surety of our eternal life. How can a couple prove in a court of law that they are married? They can know beyond the shadow of a doubt that they are married because there is a record. It is written down. How do I know I am saved? It is not because I preach. It is not because I try to win people to Jesus Christ. "This is the record." God wrote it. It is eternal, and it will never change. A record is a surety.

Sir James Simpson, the discoverer of chloroform, was dying. A friend came to him and said, "Sir James, what are your speculations?" He replied, "Speculations? I do not have any speculations. 'I know whom I have believed and am persuaded that he is able to keep that which I've committed unto him against that day.'" The Holy Spirit bears witness to the Son of God; he bears witness in the saint; and he bears witness through the scriptures.

19

Boldness in Prayer

1 John 5:14–15

I. THE DIRECTION OF PRAYER
  A. Our Acceptance
  B. Our Access
  C. Our Asking
II. THE CONDITION OF PRAYER
  A. We Must Desire God's Will
  B. We Must Discern God's Will
  C. We Must Do God's Will
III. THE FRUITION OF PRAYER
  A. Assurance of the Answer
  B. Attainment of the Answer

COMING TO THE CONCLUSION OF THIS BOOK, JOHN GATHERS TOGETHER some of the themes he has dealt with throughout.

One of the most important subjects in the Christian life is prayer. If we want the blessings of God on our life, if we want to enjoy genuine fellowship with God, we have to know something of the dynamics and power of prayer.

Bible study, also an important part of the Christian life, is always tied to prayer. When I read the Bible, God talks to me.

When I pray, I talk to God. The blessings of God come down into our life as we go to him in prayer.

> O what peace we often forfeit,
> O what needless pain we bear,
> All because we do not carry
> Everything to God in prayer.

Closely coupled with the subject of prayer is the subject of confidence or boldness before the Lord. Three times previously in this book John has talked about our confidence before the Lord. In 1 John 2:28—we can have confidence before him and not be ashamed at his coming. In 1 John 3:21—we can have confidence toward God. In 1 John 4:17—we can have boldness or confidence in the day of judgment.

Boldness is a part of Christian life. One characteristic of the early Christians was their boldness. With great boldness they gave witness to the Lord Jesus Christ. They were constantly praying that God would give them boldness in their life. You and I have the privilege as children of God not only to witness to lost men and women with openness and freedom of speech, but also to approach God in prayer in a spirit of openness, talking freely to our heavenly Father. Boldness in prayer is something we can claim in our daily life. "Cast not away therefore your confidence, which hath great recompense of reward" (Hebrews 10:35).

Prayer is difficult. I have never found praying easy. The times are such that it is always a problem to have time to talk to God as we ought. The disciples of Jesus said neither "Teach us to preach" nor "Teach us to be a witness." Instead they said, "Lord, teach us to pray."

There are no Ph.D.s in the school of prayer. You enroll in the school of prayer at the beginning of your Christian life. You continue to learn about and grow in prayer all the way through your Christian life.

How is it possible for children of God to have boldness in prayer as they approach his throne? We can have boldness in prayer when we understand at least three things given in 1 John 5:14–15.

I. The Direction of Prayer

"And this is the confidence that we have in him . . . . " The preposition *in* can be translated, "This is the confidence that we have before him or toward him." It is a preposition of the most intimate contact and it means that when we engage in prayer we get very close to God.

We must understand the direction of prayer. I do not know where heaven is. I do not know how to charter a bus to heaven. I simply know that through the Lord Jesus Christ we have assurance of heaven. When Jesus prayed he lifted his eyes toward heaven and he was aware of immediate and intimate contact with God. The direction of prayer suggests several things.

A. Our Acceptance

First if we are in fellowship with God in prayer, if we are in the presence of God, this says something about our acceptance. God's face turns toward us and he listens to us when we pray. What a wonderful thing to consider. God invites us to pray. In Matthew 6:6 Jesus says, "When thou prayest, enter into thy closet, and . . . shut thy door, . . . thy Father which seeth in secret shall reward thee openly." When we pray we are invited by God to talk to him, to enter into his presence. Countless verses in the Bible encourage and challenge us to pray.

In the Song of Solomon 2:14 Solomon says to his beloved, "O my dove, that art in the clefts of the rock, in the secret places of the stairs, let me see thy countenance, let me hear thy voice; for sweet is thy voice, and thy countenance is comely." God also speaks to redeemed souls, urging his children to pray. He longs for us to pray. When we do not pray, when we let a day go by in our life that we do not go into the presence of God, it grieves him. He misses our countenance, the sound of our voice.

We have a God to whom we can go and be accepted. "Having therefore, brethren, boldness to enter into the holiest by the blood of Jesus . . . " (Hebrews 10:19). Jesus has opened up the way into the throne room of God. Psalm 65:2 says, "O thou that hearest prayer, unto thee shall all flesh come." When I understood this truth, when I came to see that I was talking to one who accepts me, it changed my concept of prayer. I am talking to a

God who has manifested himself to me as my Father. I am his child through the new birth and my experience with the Lord Jesus Christ. Prayer then is not an attempt to overcome the reluctance of God but rather it is an effort to lay hold of God's willingness to enter our life.

B. Our Access

Second, you and I have the privilege of walking into the presence of the God of this universe. I consider my position in this world, my relationship to this created universe. The Bible says in the book of Isaiah that we are like a drop in the bucket. We are like a speck of dust on the seashore. Though we are so insignificant, "Let us . . . come boldly unto the throne of grace, that we may obtain mercy, and find grace to help in time of need" (Hebrews 4:16).

You and I do not have access to many of the important people in this world. We could sit in their office for a lifetime and we would never be able to see them. But we do have access to God. Romans 5:2 says, ". . . by whom also we have access by faith into this grace wherein we stand." We have access to God because he has opened the door.

C. Our Asking

Third, "And this is the confidence that we have in him, that, if we ask any thing according to his will, he heareth us" (1 John 5:14). If we ask, God hears. That is the Bible's simplest definition of prayer. Prayer is asking God. Prayer, of course, is many other things. Sometimes it is praise. It is wonderful to be in the presence of God, not to ask him for a single thing, but just to praise and adore him. Prayer is thanksgiving. We come into God's presence and thank him for answers to prayer, for our salvation, for material blessings. But mainly, prayer is making our requests known to God.

If prayer is asking, it means that prayer is definite. One reason our prayers are not answered is that we are so indefinite. We say, "We pray that you will save the lost people in the world." Or, "We pray that you will bless us and be with us in the service." If God answered your prayer, would you know it?

II. The Condition of Prayer

Certain laws govern answers to prayer. God gives us certain guidelines in the Bible and we must bring them into play when we pray. Matthew 21:22 says, "Whatsoever ye shall ask in prayer, believing, ye shall receive." Believing is an important part of answered prayer. We must believe that God hears us. Jesus said, "All things are possible to him that believeth." The man to whom he was speaking burst into tears. "Lord, I believe. Help thou mine unbelief" (Mark 9:24). We must believe God. That is one of the conditions of prayer, one of the laws that govern answered prayer.

Another condition of prayer is in John 14:14. Whatsoever we ask in his name he will give to us. We must pray in the name of Jesus. When we pray we must be able to say, "Father, I believe that this prayer is a prayer that Jesus would pray."

Another condition of prayer is in John 15:7. "If ye abide in me, and my words abide in you, ye shall ask what ye will, and it shall be done unto you." We have to be in fellowship with the Lord. If we are not right with God, if there is known sin in our life, then God will not hear our prayer. "If I regard iniquity in my heart, the Lord will not hear me" (Psalm 66:18).

John says, "And this is the confidence that we have in him, that, if we ask anything according to his will, he heareth us." The *anything* is contingent on the phrase, "according to his will." God will answer any prayer that is in accordance with his will.

A. We Must Desire God's Will

One guideline for praying in the will of God is to desire the will of God. We must want God's will in our life more than anything else in all the world. Jesus said, "I have come to do thy will, O God," and, "My meat is to do the will of him that sent me" (John 4:34). He desired the will of God. We Christians ought to desire the will of God because God's will is what is best for our life. Romans 12:2 says, "Be not conformed to this world: but be ye transformed by the renewing of your mind, that ye may prove what is that good, and acceptable, and perfect, will of God." We ought to be willing to say to God, "God, you know what is best. I want your will because that is what is best for my life. You know more than I know about it. You are all-wise; my wisdom is limited. I desire your will."

B. We Must Discern God's Will

When you pray and ask God for something, how do you know it is God's will? Colossians 1:9 says that it is possible for us to "be filled with the knowledge of his will."

There are two basic guidelines for knowing the will of God. First, there is the teaching of the word of God. God's will is revealed in his word. God shows us his best and his desires for us in his word. I do not mean that every time you pray you go directly to the Bible and God will give you a clear-cut verse from scripture to tell you exactly what his will is in a specific situation.

That may occur, of course. Sometimes that is exactly what God does. But as we study God's word daily, as we allow its teachings and principles to be basic to our life, we will be able to discern the will of God in particular situations.

Occasionally people come to me for counsel, and most of the time they already have their mind made up about what they want to do. They want the preacher just to endorse what they are planning. From time to time people say, "This is what I am going to do; this is what I think I ought to do," even though their plans are in clear violation of God's word. Listen, my brothers and sisters, God's will for your life will never contradict the teachings of God's word. You discern the will of God as you study the word of God.

Second, as you pray and as you surrender your will to the will of the Lord, the Holy Spirit will guide you into his will for your life. The Holy Spirit "maketh intercession for the saints according to the will of God" (Romans 8:27). Somehow the Holy Spirit puts an impression on your heart. The Holy Spirit takes his word, makes it real in your life, and gives you a definite promise, assurance, or direction. Then when you seek the will of God, when you discern the will of God and submit your will to God's will, you can know that God will answer your prayer.

C. We Must Do God's Will

In his model prayer Jesus said, "Thy will be done in earth, as it is in heaven" (Matthew 6:10). If God should clearly make known his will to your life right now, would you do it? Would you instantly obey God's will? You say, "Well now, I am not so sure. I am not really sure I want to do that. I must find out what all its implications are."

God's will is not like a cafeteria line with a wide selection of possible choices. You say, "I don't like that one; I'll take this one." A lot of people think that God lays out his will for our consideration and if it suits us, if it is consistent with what we want to do, we may say, "I will do the will of God." But Jesus says in John 7:17, "If any man will do his will, he shall know of the doctrine, whether it be of God, or whether I speak of myself." You have to be willing to do God's will. There must be total surrender to the will of God, whatever that will may be. Prayer is a mighty instrument for getting God's will done on earth.

III. The Fruition of Prayer

In 1 John 5:15 the word *know* occurs twice. "And if we know that he hear us, whatsoever we ask, we know that we have the petitions [the requests] that we desired of him." Those two occurrences of the word *know* give us two truths about the fruition of prayer.

A. Assurance of the Answer

We know that he hears us. When we have prayed according to the will of God, met the conditions, and surrendered to the will of God, we have the assurance that God will hear our prayers.

A man traveling in China went into a beautiful temple dedicated to hideous idols. There he saw a throng of worshipers taking pieces of paper on which something had been written, folding them up, and then with mud making a ball and throwing the mudballs at the idols. The traveler asked the guide about the meaning of this. "These people are writing out their prayers to their god. If it sticks to the statue, their god hears their prayer; if it does not stick, their god does not hear their prayer."

We serve a God who gives us assurance that when we ask in Jesus' name, when we ask believing, when we are in fellowship with him, and when we ask according to the will of God, we can know that our prayers are going to be answered.

B. Attainment of the Answer

The second *know* in 1 John 5:15 points to the attainment of answers to our prayers. John says we know we have the petitions we have asked of him. God answers our prayers in at least four ways.

1. Sometimes the answer to prayer is direct. Jeremiah 33:3 says, "Call unto me, and I will answer thee, and shew thee great and mighty things, which thou knowest not." Isaiah 65:24 says, "Before they call, I will answer." Sometimes God's answer comes direct from heaven. Often God answers right on the spot. In Genesis 24 the servant was seeking a bride for Isaac. He came to the well of water and began to pray something like this: O God, I want you to lead me to the one to be the bride for my master and I pray that you will send the one that I am to take back to my master. The Bible says that before he was through praying, God sent the answer.

2. Sometimes God delays his answers. In Isaiah 30:18 we read, "And therefore will the Lord wait, that he may be gracious unto you." There are blessings in God's delays. In John 11, when Mary and Martha were alarmed because of the sickness of their brother Lazarus, they sent word to Jesus. "Lord, behold, he whom thou lovest is sick." Nonetheless, Jesus stayed three days right where he was and their brother died. Were their hearts filled with doubt? They had asked for a definite thing, and the answer did not come. What did Jesus say? "This sickness is not unto death, but for the glory of God, that the Son of God might be glorified thereby." So, it may be that the reason God has not answered your prayer is in order to display something of his greater glory that can be seen through that period of suffering.

3. Sometimes God's answers are different. Sometimes we ask and God grants, but with a substitute.

Children live from one Christmas to the next. I don't know how your children are, but my children tell me what they want next Christmas on December 26. Suppose you are a little fellow and you say to Daddy, "Daddy, I want you to give me a little bicycle, not a big bicycle—all I need is just a little one." Suppose when Christmas Day comes, instead of just a little, plain, simple bicycle, you get a super-deluxe ten-speed bicycle. You did not get exactly what you asked for, but a loving father substituted something better.

God does that in our prayers. In our limited vision and in our small faith, we ask God for some little thing when he wants us to ask him for a big thing. In Psalm 2:8 God opened up the world to us when he said, "Ask of me, and I shall give thee the heathen for thine inheritance, and the uttermost parts of the earth for thy possession."

A man made an enormous request of Napoleon and to the amazement of the entire army the request was granted. Napoleon was asked, "Why did you grant such a request as this?" Napoleon replied, "He honored me by its magnitude."

4. Sometimes God's answer is a denial. God hears every prayer we pray, but sometimes God says no. Perhaps God has something else he wants to do in our life. God always does what is best.

A man was shipwrecked on an island and he began to try to flag down ships as they came by, to no avail. Every time a ship came by he would get out with his tattered shirt and wave it, trying to attract a ship to rescue him. He built himself a little hut for protection from the elements. He found some game and other food to preserve his life. The little hut was all he had.

One day he saw a ship coming. He went running down to the beach, took off his old shirt, and began to use it as a flag to signal. He shouted and waved, but the ship went on by. Forlorn, he turned and saw his little hut engulfed in flames. He said, "Oh, how terrible! The only thing I had is gone. What am I going to do?" About that time he heard the horn on the ship blowing. He ran down to the beach and there were men to rescue him. "I didn't think you saw my signal," he said. "Not see your signal? We could see a fire and smoke like that for miles." You see, the answer to his request came in a different form.

20

Sin unto Death
1 John 5:16–17

I. THE POSSIBILITY
  A. Christian Observation
  B. Christian Intercession
  C. Christian Restoration
II. THE PROHIBITION
  A. Caution
  B. Correction

"IF ANY MAN SEE HIS BROTHER SIN A SIN WHICH IS NOT UNTO DEATH, HE shall ask, and he shall give him life for them that sin not unto death. There is a sin unto death: I do not say that he shall pray for it. All unrighteousness is sin: and there is a sin not unto death" (1 John 5:16–17). Here John continues his discussion of prayer and deals with one unusual aspect.

In 1 Timothy 2:1, we read "I exhort therefore, that, first of all, supplications, prayers, intercessions, and giving of thanks, be made for all men." Here are four words that describe various aspects of prayer. Sometimes prayer is simply talking to God. At other times we make supplications, asking God for specific things. Often prayer is giving thanks to God for answered prayer. But the third of these words, intercession, or a

Christian praying for other people, has to do with these two verses in 1 John.

Our Savior has been engaged for over two thousand years in a ministry of prayer. We know a great deal about the earthly ministry of our Lord. Jesus preached three and a half years on earth, healed the sick, raised the dead, gave sight to the blind, and spent many hours in prayer. But the Bible also tells us that our Savior ascended to heaven and is presently engaged in a ministry of intercessory prayer. Hebrews 7:25 says, "Wherefore he is able also to save them to the uttermost that come unto God by him, seeing he ever liveth to make intercession for them." In Romans 8:34 we are told, "Who is he that condemneth? It is Christ that died, yea rather, that is risen again, who is even at the right hand of God, who also maketh intercession for us."

Jesus Christ is praying for every one of us. It ought to encourage us to know that we do not have to live in our own strength. We have an advocate in our heart, the Holy Spirit, who gives us power to live from within. We have an advocate with the Father, the Lord Jesus Christ, who makes requests for us and intercedes at the throne of God on our behalf. The Bible further teaches that Christians can enter into a wonderful ministry on behalf of others, the ministry of intercession.

Revelation 1:6 says, "[He] hath made us kings and priests." We are an eternal priesthood. We are a priesthood privileged to go to God on behalf of others. We can offer up spiritual sacrifices. Our prayers have efficacy before the throne of God as we pray for other people. Most of us need a great deal of improvement in this area of the Christian life. We need to be diligent in our prayers for one another.

In 1 Thessalonians 5:25 Paul admonished the Thessalonians, "Brethren, pray for us." He needed the prayers of other people just as you and I need others to pray for us.

I am afraid that we tend to be selfish in our prayers. We pray for the things we want and fail to pray for the needs of others.

God wants us to pray for other people, to be committed to a ministry of prayer. Ephesians 6:18 says we are to pray "with all prayer and supplication in the Spirit, and watching thereunto with all perseverance and supplications for all saints." James 5:16 says, "Confess your faults one to another, and pray one for another, that ye may be healed." God takes the prayers of his believing children and uses them to be a blessing in the life of others.

Our text has to do with intercessory prayer as it relates to the matter of sin in the life of other believers. Here we see a two-fold division of sin. There is a sin not unto death and there is a sin unto death. Lest we get the idea, however, that some sins are not serious, verse 17 says, "All unrighteousness is sin." There is no attempt to minimize any act of sin. John is not saying that some sins are unimportant.

One of the tragedies of American life is the loss of an awareness of sin. We have failed to understand that the wages of sin is death; the soul that sins shall die. God's judgment is on any nation that fails to understand the seriousness of sin. May we never forget that sin is a reproach to any nation. All sin is serious. All sin had to be atoned for at the cross.

I. The Possibility

"If any man see his brother sin a sin which is not unto death, he shall ask, and he shall give him life for them that sin not unto death." In that statement we see two progressive truths.

A. Christian Observation

If any man see his brother sin a sin, that is Christian observation. The Bible does not say, if any man hears that his brother has sinned. . . . John is not talking about gossip or rumor.

One of the most damaging things in the church is the practice of spreading rumors about other people—telling what you heard someone did, telling what you heard someone say, and you do not know it to be true. The favorite indoor sport of some Christians is carrying tales. Many innocent people have been hurt by the words of Christians who repeat what they have been told. John is not talking about that.

When God saved us he put us in a big family, and we are all in this Christian life together. We become brothers and sisters in Christ. God intends for Christian people to get together, not to live in isolation from one another. There is something I am able to contribute to your Christian life that will cause you to grow in the Lord. There is something you are able to contribute to my

Christian life that will make me a more mature child of God. We need one another. Because this is true we are able to see one another's failures and faults. If you are close to a person, and are able to observe their life at close range over a period of time, you will discover areas in their life where they need to grow.

Observe the finest Christian you know. He or she may be the most mature Christian you know. Stay with that man or woman long enough, observe every area of his or her life and you will discover faults. They do some things they ought not to do. The Lord did not make anyone perfect at salvation. All of us sin, all of us do things we ought not to do: a wrong habit, a wrong word, a wrong disposition, a wrong attitude—things that hurt our testimony for Jesus Christ.

We come in contact with others and we see them sin. Have you noticed how easy that is? It is not hard at all for us to see sin in the life of another person. I find it very easy to scrutinize the life of other Christians and see things in their life that ought not to be. I am quite expert at it! But I have a much harder time seeing the sins in my own life. How often we are unkind in our criticisms of other people.

B. Christian Intercession

What do you do when you see a brother sin? What is your reaction when you see another Christian do something he ought not to do? Do you pick up the phone and call nine other Christians and tell them about it? Or do you say, "I didn't think he was going to last in the first place. I didn't have a lot of confidence in him when he joined the church. I knew it would be just a matter of time." There is a tendency on the part of some Christians to become very critical and condemn those who sin.

There seems to be a "cult of the superspiritual," people who enjoy spending their time engaging in hurtful and harmful criticism and talking about other Christians who sin. Rather, we ought to think, "There, but for the grace of God, go I." We are in no position to pass judgment on any other Christian. We do not know the total situation. We do not know their background or how far they were in sin when Jesus Christ rescued them. It is totally un-Christian to have a critical spirit, to have an attitude of condemnation, toward those we see who sin.

The Christian attitude is intercession. The Christian way is to go to God in prayer. If you are going to talk about another Christian, do your talking on your knees.

One thing that hindered Simon Peter from being what he ought to be was the spiritual pride in his life. Jesus said to him, "Simon, Simon, behold, Satan hath desired to have you, that he may sift you as wheat: But I have prayed for thee [he did not talk about him], that thy faith fail not: and when thou art converted, strengthen thy brethren" (Luke 22:31–32). If you see another Christian sin, the Bible says you are to go to God in intercession.

C. Christian Restoration

John says that if you will ask, if you will pray, God will give the sinning person life.

Thus, we can have a part in the ministry of Christian restoration. There are members of churches, people who have had an experience with Jesus Christ, who somehow got out of the will of God in their life. Somehow they have not grown in the Lord, they have not read the Bible as they should have read it, and they have been overtaken in a fault. Galatians 6:1 says, "Brethren, if a man be overtaken in a fault, ye which are spiritual, restore such an one in the spirit of meekness; considering thyself, lest thou also be tempted."

We have the privilege of going to God in prayer. That is the first step toward the restoration of others. The prayer of God's believing children can rescue a man or woman from losing their testimony and possibly losing their life.

We need to do a great deal more praying like this in the church. I do not know of a church anywhere that does not have a lot of members who are totally inactive. Sunday school teachers have a roll of ex-attendees who now never come. Every time you see the name of an inactive Christian, it is a reminder of your divine injunction to go to God on behalf of that person and to engage in intercessory prayer.

I am convinced that if Sunday school teachers would get on fire for Jesus Christ and really pray, they could greatly increase attendance in their class. Pray them in on Sunday! Do you spend time in prayer for the attendance of your Sunday school class? Do you one by one take those absentees to God in prayer, asking God to restore them to Christian effectiveness?

II. THE PROHIBITION

The second statement is: "There is a sin unto death." John says, "I do not say that he shall pray for it." Entwined in that statement is the prohibition of intercessory prayer. God is saying through John that there are some situations where prayer is prohibited.

A. Caution

First, a word of caution. The *a* should not be in the verse; it is misleading. It gives the idea that John is talking about a specific act of sin. It would be better translated as: "There is sin leading to or leaning toward, moving in the direction of, death." The word of God states unequivocally that there is a condition of heart and soul and spirit that can result in death. John is not talking about a specific act of sin necessarily, but a condition of heart, an attitude or a spirit that leads toward death.

What is the sin unto death? Some believe that John is referring to spiritual death, but all sin leads to spiritual death. In Genesis 2:17 the Lord spoke to Adam and told him not to partake of the tree of the knowledge of good and evil. God said, "In the day that thou eatest thereof thou shalt surely die." Yet Adam lived hundreds of years after that. God did not mean he would surely die physically that day. Although he did not die physically, he died spiritually. He became a fallen creature, a man in need of a Savior. All sin leads to spiritual death.

Allow known sin to stay in your heart and it will kill your spiritual testimony. One of the greatest hindrances to the effectiveness of the witnessing efforts of any church is the open sin in the life of its members. We are fooling ourselves to believe that God is going to bless any church when there are members in the church who have open sin in their life. Sin will kill the spiritual life of a Christian; it will kill the spirituality of a church.

Others believe that the sin unto death is "the unpardonable sin." The Bible talks about an unpardonable sin. Jesus Christ says, "And whosoever speaketh a word against the Son of man, it shall be forgiven him: but whosoever speaketh against the Holy Ghost, it shall not be forgiven him" (Matthew 12:32). There is an unpardonable sin, but it can be committed only by a lost person. If you are saved, it is impossible to commit the unpardonable sin. There are people in mental institutions because they think they have committed the unpardonable sin. I have talked to Christians who are deeply troubled because they think they have committed the unpardonable sin. I talked to a man who had gone through some traumatic experiences. He had become involved with an extremist religious sect, but because he did not join, they ingrained in his mind that he had committed the unpardonable sin. If you have any fear that you have committed the unpardonable sin, that is proof positive you have not committed it. A Christian cannot commit the unpardonable sin.

What is meant here then? I believe John means that there is sin leading to physical death. This is the word of caution to us as Christians. It is possible for a Christian so to continue in an attitude of rebellion against God and to allow sin to dwell in his life, hindering the testimony and effectiveness of his church, that God will take his physical life. God will give him a dishonorable discharge. God will send him on to glory ahead of time. He will be saved "so as by fire," but he will suffer loss (1 Corinthians 3:15).

There are examples of this in the Bible. Moses committed sin unto death. Moses was perhaps the greatest personality in the Old Testament—Moses the great man of God, Moses the prophet who was called by God to go down into Egypt and lead his children out of the land Egypt. Is it not amazing that Moses was used of God to lead the children of Israel all the way through the wilderness, yet Moses himself did not enter the promised land? Moses was pastor of a "church" with two and a half million members, and all of them were backslidden except two, Joshua and Caleb.

Every time something went wrong they blamed Moses. But Moses was patient; he prayed and prayed.

Eventually, however, even Moses' patience grew thin. It is so easy to let the behavior of other people cause us to falter in our Christian walk. Moses got mad and did not obey God completely. Then God said, "Moses, because you have not obeyed me fully you will not enter Canaan. In fact, you are going to die ahead of time." This was sin unto death.

Why was God so severe on Moses? James 3:1 says, "My brethren, be not many masters, knowing that we shall receive the greater condemnation." The greater the light God has given you, the greater the position of leadership he has placed you in, the greater your responsibility to be totally dedicated to the will of God. To whom much is given much is required (Luke 12:48).

There is a second illustration in the Old Testament. Achan committed sin unto death. He took the Babylonian garments, the silver and the wedge of gold. He disobeyed the Lord completely. When God called Israel to a screeching halt, Joshua fell on his knees before God in agony. God said, "Get on your feet. Joshua, there is sin in the camp." It was Achan. He was stoned to death.

Perhaps you reply, "Well, that was in the Old Testament; that was under law." What happens under grace? In Acts 5 there was a couple whose life was hindering the testimony of their church. They pretended a dedication they did not possess. They lied to the Holy Spirit. When Simon Peter asked them about their dedication, they lied. When they lied, they died! God put them to death because their sin hindered the church. In 1 Corinthians 11:30 we are told, "For this cause many are weak and sickly among you, and many sleep."

In 1 Corinthians 5:5 God told about a man who was living in open sin. Paul said, "To deliver such an one unto Satan for the destruction of the flesh, that the spirit may be saved in the day of the Lord Jesus." It is possible for Christians so to sin against light and so to persist in a life of disobedience to the will of God, that they can commit a sin unto death.

B. Correction

John says, Do not pray for them. Leave them alone.

I do not know when that time comes. I think we ought to pray as much as we can pray for other Christians. Sometimes, however, you persist in prayer, and God seems to stop you. I do not know when it comes, but somewhere along the way there comes a time when God may say, It is enough. In Jeremiah 7:16

God says, "Therefore pray not thou for this people, neither lift up cry nor prayer for them, neither make intercession to me: for I will not hear thee." God said, "It is too late to pray."

God revealed to Abraham that Sodom and Gomorrah were going to be destroyed with fire. Abraham had implored God six times, and begged him to spare them. The sixth time it was too late to pray.

Christian, do not flirt with God; you are playing with fire. Do not pretend a piety you do not possess. Do not pretend to be what you are not. Do not presume on the mercy of God because the scriptures teach that there comes a time when God says, It is enough.

21

A Trinity of Certainty
1 John 5:18–21

I. CHRISTIAN POWER
   A. Expressed
   B. Explained
   C. Exhibited
II. CHRISTIAN POSITION
   A. Certainty
   B. Contrast
III. CHRISTIAN PERCEPTION
   A. Origin
   B. Object

THE BOOK OF 1 JOHN IS THE BOOK OF CHRISTIAN CERTAINTY. GOD LAID IT ON the heart of John to write this short letter so that we might never be in the dark about matters crucial to our soul's salvation.

God wants every one of us to know that we are saved, to have a surety that cannot be shaken, an assurance that cannot be moved. We have seen in this study that certainty of salvation is possible because of what God has said to us in his word. "And this is the record, that God hath given to us eternal life, and this life is in his Son" (1 John 5:11). We have the word of God, a firm foundation on which to build our certitude and confidence.

When a child of God comes to understand that his or her salvation does not depend on feelings or on self-effort, but on what God has done in Christ; when he or she accepts what God has to say about that, then assurance comes. Then we are able to sing, "My faith has found a resting place . . . the written Word of God." Our knowledge of salvation is firmly established on the impregnable rock of holy scripture.

God wants us to know certain things. Over and over we have seen John use the word *know.* And so, as if to summarize, he concludes this letter with three tremendous certainties, a trinity of certainty. We can say with certainty, "I know these things because God has given me divine insight and knowledge."

There are many things we do not know, of course. Some things we can never fully understand in this life. However, some things we can know, and we ought not to let the things we know be disturbed by the things we do not know.

I. CHRISTIAN POWER

In verse 18 John speaks about the power available to the child of God, power to give victory over sin.

A. Expressed

"We know that whosoever is born of God sinneth not" (1 John 5:18). Again, John is not saying that a Christian never commits an act of sin, which is not true. It would contradict what John himself said in the first chapter. Here the Bible uses the present tense of the verb. If we are born of God we do not make a habit of sin; we do not constantly, continually, habitually sin.

This is the difference the new-birth experience makes in the life of an individual. Before a person comes to know Christ and is born into the family of God, the trend and direction of his life is toward sin. He really has no choice about the matter. He sins because it is his nature. Then the wonderful experience of the new birth comes to pass. He is born of God and when that happens the trend is reversed. He does not make a habit of sin. We Christians may sin occasionally, but we will not sin habitually.

Through the Lord Jesus Christ, Christians have power over sin. Salvation delivers us not only from the penalty of sin in our past, the presence of sin in the future, but salvation brings to our disposal the power over sin in the present, in daily life. Although you may sin as a Christian, it is not necessary that you do so. The lost person has no choice about the matter. The child of God does have a choice. We can choose not to sin; we can refuse to be shackled by the bondage of sin. We do not have to lead a defeated life.

B. Explained

"But he that is begotten of God keepeth himself." That statement may give the impression that it is the child of God who keeps himself. But that is not the correct meaning of the verse. The reference is not to the child of God but to the Lord Jesus Christ. "He that is begotten of God" is a reference to Jesus. The word *himself* should be translated "him." "He [Jesus] that is begotten of God keepeth him [the child of God]." This expresses our new power. It is not that we have the power to overcome sin, but Jesus keeps us and gives us power over sin.

You and I are no more able to keep ourselves than we are able to save ourselves. Everything we have comes from the Lord Jesus Christ. We are saved and kept by his grace. We "are kept by the power of God through faith unto salvation ready to be revealed in the last time" (1 Peter 1:5).

Jesus Christ has us in his hands. In John 10:28 Jesus says, "And I give unto them eternal life; and they shall never perish, neither shall any man pluck them out of my hand."

We reach out to him. We hold onto him in love, confidence, and trust, but the Lord Jesus Christ has us in his hand. In John 17:12 Jesus says, "Those that thou gavest me I have kept, and none of them is lost, but the son of perdition." Second Timothy 1:12 says, "I know whom I have believed, and am persuaded that he is able to keep that which I have committed unto him against that day." Jude 24 says, "Now unto him that is able to keep you from falling, and to present you faultless before the presence of his glory with exceeding joy . . ." Power over sin resides in the Lord Jesus Christ.

C. Exhibited

"That wicked one toucheth him not" (1 John 5:18). The devil does not lay hold of the child of God. The devil cannot get the child of God in his grasp. The good news of the gospel is that Jesus Christ has released us from the bondage of Satan. You are not the hopeless victim of the devil.

There used to be a little phrase going around, "The devil made me do it." We have laughed about that. But if you are a lost person you can truthfully say, "The devil made me do it." If you are a child of God you cannot truthfully say, "The devil made me do it." The devil has no power over you beyond the power you give him. The Bible says, "Neither give place to the devil" (Ephesians 4:27).

II. CHRISTIAN POSITION

First, we see the certainty of our position. "And we know that we are of God." Second, we see a contrast. "And the whole world lieth in wickedness."

A. Certainty

We know that we originate from God. We know that the source of our spiritual life is God. There are only two locations spiritually. That person who is born of human nature is born into the Adam family, born in sin. If anyone is born only one time and lives life only with that one nature and dies, the Bible says that such persons die in their sin.

Through the new birth we receive the nature of God. "But as many as received him, to them gave he power to become the sons of God, even to them that believe on his name: Which were born, not of blood, nor of the will of the flesh, nor of the will of man, but of God" (John 1:12–13). Colossians 3:3 says we are "hid with Christ in God."

There is no reason for a Christian to be defeated. I am in God, in the heavenly Father, in Christ, in the Son, in the Holy Spirit of God. Everything God is, I have at my disposal.

B. Contrast

On the other hand, the whole world lies in the domain, lies prostrate, in the power of the wicked one, the devil. I think we would know *that* even if the Bible did not say it. Something is wrong with this world. This is a fallen, vicious world and we ought not to be surprised at anything we see in it. It is not going to get better, because the devil, the prince of this world, is in charge of the governments of this world. He is in charge of the secular educational systems of this world. He is in charge of the non-Christian religions of this world.

The world has its opinions and insists that you also have those opinions. This world has its mold and insists that you conform to its mold. Christians who refuse to do so are going to have problems along the way.

If you are a young person in high school, that high school has its mold. That high school wants you to be just like it is. If you dare to be a Christian, you are going to encounter problems.

Or you grownups, go to the place where you work, and that work has its mold. Our entire society has its way of doing things. When you dare to be different, when you dare to live like a person who is born of God, you are going to run into problems. This world is not a child of grace to lead us on to God.

III. CHRISTIAN PERCEPTION

As Christians we have been given spiritual insight. "And we know that the Son of God is come, and hath given us an understanding." The "understanding" John refers to is spiritual perception.

A. Origin

Here is the origin of our perception: "The Son of God is come." Our Savior has arrived in our heart and is there to stay.

There are two incarnations of the Lord Jesus. The first was a historical incarnation that took place two thousand years ago. But the Bible also teaches an incarnation of Jesus Christ in the individual heart, experientially. Christ, living in our heart, has brought spiritual perception. God gives the child of God the capacity to understand spiritual things. We are able to perceive things that those outside of Christ are not able to perceive.

I was talking to a lost man recently, a very intelligent man who is searching. He said to me, "I don't know what the problem is. I am reading the Bible, I am studying the Bible, and it makes no sense to me whatsoever. I read it but I don't understand it. I open it up and it means nothing to me whatsoever." Why? First Corinthians 2:14 says, "But the natural man receiveth not the things of the Spirit of God: for they are foolishness unto him: neither can he know them, because they are spiritually discerned."

Ephesians 1:18 says that the eyes of your understanding must be enlightened. God has to give you a new set of eyes. With all of your brilliance, regardless of your IQ, you will never be able to understand spiritual things until God gives you spiritual eyes. We are told about the disciples of Jesus in Luke 24:45,"Then opened he their understanding, that they might understand the scriptures."

Remember the story of the man who was blind until Jesus came by and touched his eyes, and then he saw things he had never seen before? People began to pick on him, tried to get explanations, and tried to get him to say that Jesus was a sinner. Finally the man said, "Well, whether he is a sinner or not, I do not know: but this one thing I know, whereas I was blind, now I see!"

Why is it that there was a time in your life when you would not have been caught dead in a church? Why are you now reading this book, doing everything you can to learn as much as possible about the Bible? I will tell you why. God has given you understanding, he has given you perception, and that makes all the difference.

We see the difference it makes in 2 Kings 5, the story of Naaman the leper. Leprosy is a "type" of sin. Naaman, who had leprosy, came to Israel in order to find a cure. When he got there, Elisha the man of God told him to take seven dips in the river Jordan. Naaman was looking at the situation from a natural point of view. A lot of people are like that.

It is God, however, who sets up the terms of salvation. You say, "That is mighty dogmatic." That's right. You either accept it and are saved or you reject it and are lost.

Naaman had figured out how he was going to be healed. When Elisha said, "Take seven dips in the river Jordan," "Naaman was wroth." It made him mad, "And he went away, and said, Behold, I thought, He will surely come out to me, and stand, and call on the name of the Lord his God, and strike his hand over the place, and recover the leper" (2 Kings 5:11). But

Naaman was willing to submit to the command of God. "And he returned to the man of God, he and all his company, and came, and stood before him: and he said, Behold now I know" (2 Kings 5:15). What a difference. God had given him understanding.

There is a lot of difference between what we think and what we know. "I thought salvation was this way; now I know!" The origin of our perception is from the Lord Jesus Christ. He has come into our heart and has given us spiritual eyes.

B. Object

Why does God give us spiritual eyes? John says, "That we may know him that is true," that we may know God who is real.

Do you want to know God? Do you want to know the God who is real? Scripture goes on to say, "We are in him that is true, even in his Son Jesus Christ. This is the true God." Who? Jesus. Jesus is the true God. You meet God in Jesus Christ and the only way to God is Jesus Christ.

Not many roads lead to God. Not many avenues lead to salvation. Jesus says, "I am the way, the truth, and the life: no man cometh unto the Father, but by me" (John 14:6).

A man came up to a Bible conference speaker one night and said, "I think this salvation is kind of like a fellow who gets in an airport and he wants to go from Philadelphia to New York. Different airlines can take you from Philadelphia to New York. I might get on Eastern and go to New York. I might get on Delta and go to New York. I might get on United and go to New York. I think there are many routes to get to heaven." The Bible teacher replied, "Yes, sir, you are right. There are many airlines that will get you from Philadelphia to New York, but we are not talking about an airplane ride. We are talking about getting to heaven." God says there is only one way, and the only way to meet the true God is in Jesus Christ. The only way we find reality is when we meet reality in the Lord Jesus Christ.

John ends his letter rather abruptly. "Little children, keep yourselves from idols" (1 John 5:21), a command that seems to be altogether detached from what he has just said. At close examination, however, we discover that it is intimately connected. He has just said, "Reality is in Jesus Christ," and

therefore "Watch yourselves, guard yourselves, keep yourselves from unreality. Keep yourselves from idols."

The word *idol* means "that which is seen." An idol is any substitute for God. You can make an idol of your job. You can make
an idol of money. You can make an idol of your talents. You can
make an idol of your clothes, your car, your house, your family.
Anything that comes between you and God is an idol—and is
unreal. When it comes to the end and you call on your idol,
there will be no reply because that idol is unreal.

A lot of people say, "It doesn't matter what you believe, just as
long as you are sincere." It does matter what we believe. You
can be sincere but if you do not go God's way, you are not right. I
read in the paper about a tragedy that occurred with a salt
shaker. Several people died because what they thought was salt
in a salt shaker was not salt at all but a poison that looked just
like salt. They sincerely thought they were eating salt, but they
were eating poison. Do you have reality? Have you come to Jesus
Christ? Can you say, "I know"?

2 JOHN

22

Love in the Truth
2 John 1–13

I. Introduction
II. Truth and Love Must Be Practiced
III. Truth and Love Can Be Perverted

THE SECOND EPISTLE OF JOHN MAY BE THE MOST NEGLECTED BOOK IN THE New Testament. I have never heard a sermon on 2 John, although I have taught it a few times.

God used the apostle John as a human instrument to speak about essentials of Christian life. Three words summarize what it is all about—in its past, present, and future.

A word that describes the past is *faith*. By faith we receive what Jesus did for us at Calvary's cross two thousand years ago. In his gospel, John writes about faith in Jesus Christ as the Son of God.

The word *love* describes what should be the present attitude of every believer. John's three letters deal specifically with the subject of love.

The word *hope* describes the outlook of Christians as we look toward the days of the future. The book of Revelation deals with hope.

So the Spirit of God used John, as he had also used Paul, to speak to us about faith, love, and hope. The little book of 2 John was written especially to help us understand what genuine love is. We must not misunderstand what love is really all about.

I. INTRODUCTION

Almost all scholars agree that this writer, the elder, is John, the beloved disciple (2 John 1). When he calls himself an elder, he is using one of the terms that described a pastor of a local congregation. In the latter days of his life, before he went home to be with the Lord, John was pastor of a congregation in Ephesus.

Whom does John intend when he says he is writing to the elect lady? One view claims that John is writing to a local church. Then later, where John says, "The children of thy elect sister greet thee" (v. 13), this view regards John as referring to a sister church sending greetings to another church. One problem with such a view is that the church is not pictured in the Bible as having children. There are no children of the church. When you receive the Lord Jesus as your Savior, you are born into the family of God. You become a child of God, not a child of the church.

A second view, which I believe is more correct, is that John is writing to a real Christian woman, someone he has known or heard about. He knows her sister who is also a believer and her sister's children. But he has also met some of the children of this "elect [chosen] lady," and seeing their devotion to the Lord, John is writing their mother a letter, commending her for the way she has brought up these children in the faith.

If this is true, 2 John is the only book in the Bible specifically addressed to a woman, and it is a commendation of a Christian mother. Here is a woman who has taught her children the truth. They are maturing in the things of God. John is refreshed, blessed, as he sees these young people.

Some time ago I visited a family who has recently moved here. I got there at supper time, and they invited me right on in. I sat down at the table with them. Then the father said, "It's time for us to have our prayer." When he did, he and his wife and his two teenage daughters held out their hands. I joined hands with them, we bowed our heads and had prayer. In the course of the visit it became obvious that this mother and father had taught the word of God to their children, had brought them up in the house of the Lord. The evidence of spiritual maturity in the life of those girls was an encouragement to me.

The letter John writes to this godly Christian woman can encourage us in our day that it is possible to bring up children to love Jesus, to live for Jesus, to serve Jesus.

It is not easy. But we have to keep in mind that John was writing in the midst of a society that was absolutely pagan and therefore was difficult in similar ways. Here is a mother who succeeded, and I want to encourage mothers today with the example of this unknown Christian mother.

We have some of the sweetest, godliest, most dedicated young people in our church I've ever seen anywhere. I believe it is largely due to the fact that each child's life has been saturated by prayer from their Christian mother and father. They have taught them the word; they have brought them to a Bible-believing church through the years. The life of each of their children is now an open testimony to the power of Christ and the influence of a Christian home.

In the first four verses of this letter, John uses the word *truth* five times. Verse 1: "I love in the truth" and "All they that have known the truth." Verse 2: "For truth's sake." Verse 3: "Truth and love." Verse 4: "Walking in truth."

John also uses the word *love* four times. When you put those two words together, you see the emphasis that John intended in this short letter. He was saying, "I want to explain to you the meaning of love. I want you to understand what Christian love is."

To love someone in the truth (v. 1) is not romantic love. It's the same thing as our saying today, "I love you in the Lord." That statement is the key to this little book.

In the third verse he closes out that greeting by saying, "In truth and love." Love and truth go together. If you take love away from truth, you don't have Christian love. One thing we hear a great deal about in Christian circles is that we all ought just to love one another, lay aside our doctrinal convictions and the things we believe in scripture, and not be so caught up in doctrine. I agree we all ought to love one another. There is too much bickering, too much division, too much strife among believers, but it is never correct to lay aside doctrine for love. Real love always operates in the sphere of the truth.

When John talks about walking in the truth, he is talking about the life of Christian believers. The Bible, the word of God, is the truth of God. The whole body of Christian truth is contained in the Bible. In the book of Revelation, when John said that no man was to add to this prophecy and no man was to take away from this prophecy, he was in effect closing the canon of scripture. So, in the pages of our Bible we have the sum, substance, and totality of Christian truth. Truth is the foundation of our faith and it is also the basis of love.

II. Truth and Love Must Be Practiced

In the body of this letter, we find two lessons about love and truth. The first one is this: Love and truth must be practiced.

What does it mean to live in truth (v. 4)? Here, *walking* means your lifestyle, your behavior, your daily life as a Christian. What characterizes those whose life is filled with God's truth? John says, I saw your children and they were living in truth. He says, I want you to understand what the commandment is. It's not anything new. The commandment is to love one another. Love and truth must be put into practice. Love and truth must characterize the lifestyle of believers.

"And this is his commandment, That we should believe on the name of his Son Jesus Christ, and love one another, as he gave us commandment" (1 John 3:23). To love one another is God's commandment. In the gospel of John, Jesus was with his disciples just before going to the cross. In the upper room he was telling them what he wanted them to do, the kind of life he wanted them to live. "A new commandment I give unto you, That ye love one another; as I have loved you, that ye also love one another. By this shall all men know that ye are my disciples, if ye have love one to another" (John 13:34–35). That is the badge, the identifying mark, of the believer—if you have love one to another.

Isn't it amazing that God has to command us to love one another? If you have ever brought up children, you understand why. If you have ever had a boy and a girl in the same house, you understand why we have to be commanded to love one another.

Have you ever said, "Listen, son, love your little sister"? This old nature of ours doesn't want to love. We talk about babies and how innocent they look. You bring that precious little darling cuddly soft bundle home, put it in a bassinet, and about two o'clock in the morning, no matter how sleepy you are, no matter how tired you are, no matter how early you have to get up in the morning, if that baby wants something to eat, he or she will wake you up and cry until being fed.

By nature we do not love others. But when a person receives the truth of Jesus in his or her heart, the love of God dwells in that heart in the person of the Holy Spirit.

Now, love is not as easy to live out as it is to talk about. "To dwell above with saints we love, that will indeed be glory; to live below with saints we know, well, that's another story." When you get down to the nitty gritty it's hard to love people.

When Jesus said these words, the disciples had just been fussing about who was going to be greatest in the kingdom of God. They were so mad at one another that when it came time to perform the common courtesy of washing feet, not a one of them would do it. Jesus had to do it.

What is love? Today there are all kinds of definitions of love, amazing definitions. Think about all the songs written about love and what they say love is. John defines love like this: "We walk after his commandments" (v. 6). Love is obeying the Lord. Real love is a choice, not an emotion. I choose to love you. When I obey, I do what God tells me to do.

What about people who never darken the door of the house of God? The only way we are going to reach them is by love, not by beating them over the head, not by condemning them. Love begets love. When we love people, we obey the commandments of the Lord and we go out in love and say, "God loves you and we love you and we want you to come and be a part of our fellowship." Truth and love must be practiced.

III. TRUTH AND LOVE CAN BE PERVERTED

In the days when John was writing this letter, wandering, vagabond teachers proliferated. They popped up everywhere and expounded all sorts of doctrines. We have to keep in mind that the entire canon of scripture had not been established at this

time. There was no New Testament as such. Some books had
been written in earlier years of the first century, but no completed New Testament existed. These wandering preachers
came and taught all kinds of digressions from the truth and per-
versions of the truth. John deals with them head-on. He says
that many deceivers have entered into the world (v. 7).

This is how you spot a deceiver, a perverter of the truth, a
false teacher. They "confess not [they deny] that Jesus Christ is
come in the flesh. This is a deceiver and an antichrist." The
Gnostics were teaching that Jesus Christ was not really a person. They believed that the body was evil. Therefore, they said,
God could not have tainted himself with a human body. Jesus
was just a phantom. Some of them went so far as to say that
when he walked he didn't even leave a footprint! You see what
such teachings do to the Christian faith. John says in the first
chapter of his gospel, "The Word [talking about the eternal
Christ] was made flesh, and dwelt among us." Jesus Christ was
the God-man and the man-God. He was as much man as if he
had not been God. He was as much God as if he had not been
man. If anyone tampers with the deity of Jesus, if anyone denies
that Christ is come in the flesh as the Savior of the world, John
says that such a one is a deceiver.

This is serious business. "Look to yourselves, that we lose not
those things which we have wrought, but that we receive a full
reward" (v. 8). John is saying, if you tamper with error and get
away from the truth, you may not lose your salvation, but you
will lose your reward. In verse 9 the word *transgresseth* means
to go forth or go beyond. The reference is to people who go beyond the doctrine of Christ, which is characteristic of every
cult. They have some new information that goes beyond the
doctrines of the word of God. Or they have a new book that's
been hidden all these years, or a revelation just discovered by
some new prophet.

Some people in this world think they are smarter than Jesus
Christ. They go beyond the teachings of the word of God. When
you go beyond what Jesus Christ had to say about anything,
you've gone too far. We may talk about liberals and modernists,
but those terms are not used in the Bible. We hear about those
who deny the virgin birth of Jesus. They deny the shed blood of
Jesus Christ on the cross. They deny salvation, by grace,

through faith. Verse 9 says that such a person "hath not God." John is saying that such persons are not saved. They need to be born again.

Watch how these false teachers operate. "If there come any unto you. . . ." (v. 10). They will go house to house. Most false cults are wrong in their head and right in their feet.

The Bible teaches us that we ought to visit. The Bible teaches us that we ought to go house to house (see Acts 20:20). It's amazing how Christians have missed that. When a church has people in it who go visiting, folks think that's an amazing thing. But that's the way it's supposed to be. That's normal Christianity.

John says this about it: "If there come any unto you, and bring not this doctrine, receive him not into your house, neither bid him God speed: For he who biddeth him God speed is partaker of his evil deeds" (vv. 10–11). You may think, "Oh, that is so harsh. That is so unloving. Oh, brother John, you don't love people."

Well, although John was called the apostle of love, an old legend describes how strong he was. Earlier I mentioned a heretic in John's day, a cultist, a false teacher named Cerinthus. One day John was at the bath house when Cerinthus arrived. John jumped out of the water, got his clothes and towels, and took off running. He said, "Let us hurry from this house, lest it fall on us. Cerinthus, the enemy of truth, is here."

We must not allow the poison of false doctrine to get in our home. We don't have to be rude or impolite about it. What would happen if every time one of those false cultists came to our door we just lovingly said to them, "I'm sorry, but we believe the word of God, and you can't come in"? What would happen if they heard that at one hundred doors a day? Might it make them wonder if perhaps they were wrong?

My son called me late one night from college. He said, "Are you asleep?" I said, "No," so we talked a while. He told me about a girl who had graduated in his high school class. She was an attractive young woman, an outstanding basketball player. In recent weeks some boys had been bothering her, so her father bought her a gun to protect herself. That weekend she and a friend were at a drive-in restaurant and the boys were there again. Jeanna picked up the gun. Her friend said, "You better be

careful with that gun." She said, "Oh, there's a safety on it. See."
She pulled the trigger and blew herself into eternity.

To be confused about the truth is deadly. Jesus *is* the truth.

3 JOHN

23

Living the Truth
3 John 1–14

I. Gaius: A Commendable Christian
II. Diotrephes: A Cantankerous Christian
III. Demetrius: A Consistent Christian

THE THIRD EPISTLE OF JOHN WAS WRITTEN TO AN INDIVIDUAL CHRISTIAN. IN it we can study three church members: Gaius, Diotrephes, and Demetrius. Those are not names you would give your sons, but in those days they were common names.

Three words are used interchangeably in the New Testament to refer to the same office in the local church: elder, bishop, and pastor. The term *pastor* means one who feeds the flock of God, the shepherd, the one who gives the sheep of God the good food of the word. The word *bishop* means an overseer or administrator. The word *elder* carries the idea of maturity and counsel. So, John the elder, the beloved apostle, is writing to a man named Gaius who is described as well beloved. We don't know who Gaius was. Although some other men in the New Testament had this name, we don't know if this Gaius is one of those. But the title John gives to Gaius is of interest.

In Matthew 3:17, God the Father spoke from heaven when Jesus was baptized and said, "This is my beloved Son, in whom I am well pleased." In Romans 1:7 Paul gave the believers in

Rome this word of greeting: "To all that be in Rome, beloved of God." In each case the same Greek word for *beloved* is used.

Jesus was the Father's beloved Son. Believers are called the beloved of God. How does that come about? Ephesians 1:6 says, ". . . to the praise of the glory of his grace, wherein he hath made us accepted in the beloved." The beloved in that verse refers to Jesus. God the Father said, This is my beloved Son. I am well pleased with him. Believers are his beloved ones. We are his children because we are accepted in Jesus. Our approval in heaven, so to speak, is on the basis of our position in Jesus. We are the beloved because we belong to Jesus. We are accepted by God on the basis of the finished work of Jesus Christ at Calvary's cross.

John is writing to a man who is a beloved one of God. Then John says, ". . . whom I love in the truth." He uses the word, *beloved*, four times in this letter (vv. 1,2,5,11).

I. GAIUS: A COMMENDABLE CHRISTIAN

This is a love letter, written from a Christian pastor to a commendable Christian man. Whenever he thought about him, John's heart welled up with love. John says to Gaius, "Beloved, I wish above all things that thou mayest prosper and be in health, even as thy soul prospers." That was a common greeting. It's the equivalent of saying today, "Dear Joe, I hope you are feeling fine. I hope you are doing well."

Notice in this greeting what John wishes for Gaius. He says to him, Gaius, I want you to prosper and be in health, even as your soul prospers. In other words, I want you to have the same kind of health physically as you have spiritually. John is paying Gaius a tremendous compliment. He is saying, You are robust spiritually, you are in spiritual health. I'm hoping you will be just as well off on the outside as you are on the inside. He is saying, Gaius, you are a dynamite Christian. You are an on-fire Christian. You are spiritually strong in the Lord.

I wonder what would happen if this kind of prayer were prayed for us and it was instantly answered. If it were, how would we be? John is talking about the importance of maintaining your inner spiritual life, keeping your soul strong.

A whole school of teaching called the health and wealth gospel is going around. This is one of the verses used to teach it. Somehow if you find the mysterious keys in scripture, if you unlock these principles in scripture, then you can have physical health and wealth—and this is an indication of God's blessing on your life. We know that God wants us to be well. We know that God wants us to *do* well. But it is not necessarily an evidence of the blessing of God on our life if we prosper financially. Do you know anybody who has prospered financially, and as a result became a strong Christian, really dedicated to the Lord? Or do you know people who have prospered financially and it has been detrimental to their spiritual life? I know a whole lot more in that condition. I know folks who were serving the Lord, living for Jesus, and they began to be blessed financially. That financial blessing then led them away from serving the Lord.

I heard a story about a man whom God was blessing. He was making $100.00 a week and he started giving God 10 percent. God began to bless him more, and then he was making $1,000.00 a week and he gave God $100.00 a week. God blessed him more, and he was making $10,000 a week. He was giving $1,000.00 a week to the Lord. Then, God gave him a million dollars a week. Do you know what the man said then? He said, "Now listen, preacher, I can't tithe anymore. That's too much money to be tithing." The preacher said, "Let's get down on our knees." They did, and he said, "Lord, bless this brother and give him $100.00 a week from now on."

Sometimes you can be so blessed financially that you get away from God. You can be backslidden and as far out of the will of God as anyone can possibly be, and still be making money hand over fist. That doesn't necessarily mean God is blessing you.

Now, if God does bless you, praise his name for it and use your money for his honor and glory.

Then, John says, I want you to be in health. God wants us to be healthy. It's important to take care of our physical body. Paul said to young Timothy, "Bodily exercise profits a little." I got into jogging a few years ago. I had started getting up in the morning feeling like I wanted to go back to bed, I was just so weary and worn out. I'd sleep eight hours and it felt like I had slept eight minutes. Here I was about thirty-eight years old, so I went to the doctor. I knew that pushing forty was pretty rough, but I didn't know it was that rough. I told the doctor, "I need some help. I'm tired, I'm dragging around, I'm worn out all the time." He said, "What kind of exercise do you do? You need to get on an exercise program." I started exercising, lost about ten pounds, and got my cardiovascular system in good shape. I found out I had more energy than I ever had before. I could accomplish more, and my mind was clearer than it had ever been. It helps our spiritual life to get our physical life in shape. The body and soul are so close to one another that if the body is run down, it affects our spiritual life.

But the main thing John is saying is this: Be sure to keep your inner life the way it ought to be. Stay strong in your heart with the Lord.

"For I rejoiced greatly, when the brethren came and testified of the truth that is in thee, even as thou walkest in the truth" (v. 3). Some folks had come from where Gaius was and had given John a report that the truth was in Gaius, that is, he was learning the truth. He was also walking in the truth, living the truth. John says: "I have no greater joy than to hear that my children walk in truth" (v. 4).

This is an indication that John had won Gaius to the Lord. John, the faithful pastor, getting a good report about one of his converts, is filled with joy. If you want to bring joy to the heart of your pastor or elders, live for Jesus. Serve Jesus.

John moves on, specifically commending Gaius (vv. 5-8). Here's the background of what he is saying. In those days, when Christian evangelists and preachers traveled, when Christian teachers went from church to church and from place to place to teach the word of God, they didn't have motels and hotels to stay in. John couldn't write and say, "I'm coming over to Ephesus and I'll be checking in at the Holiday Inn and will be conducting meetings." They did have inns, but they were often dirty and infected with fleas and varmints of all descriptions. Further, there was such immorality in those inns that they just weren't a desirable place to stay. Because of that, Christian families opened their home to these traveling missionaries.

Gaius was the kind of Christian who had opened up his home like that. He had been so faithful, such a gracious host, that as these brethren came through to where John was, they said, "There is a man, Gaius, in this church, who extends Christian hospitality and he is a great blessing." Now John is writing and saying, I've been hearing about what you are doing, that you are faithful in extending Christian hospitality. You have brought these people forward on their journey in a manner worthy of God. In other words, you have extended God-like grace to these people.

John is dealing with the matter of supporting those who teach and preach the word of God. Here we see three basic statements about the need of Christians to support Christian workers. First, it is a God-like thing to do. Second, when men are on a mission for Jesus' sake, Christians are responsible for their support so that they do not make any appeal to the non-Christian community. They should take "nothing of the Gentiles." They do not derive their support from the lost world. It is the responsibility of God's people to support God's work. We don't make appeals for money in our church's television ministry. When we do visitation and outreach, we do not ask for money. We don't go out selling things.

I remember when I was pastor of a little country church, we were getting ready to build Sunday school rooms. Some of the women came to me and said, "We want to help raise some money for the building. We would like to get vanilla extract, sell it in the community, take the proceeds, and give it to our church." I was just a young pastor and I said, "Let me talk to the people about giving. Let me preach about giving to the Lord's work and let's see if we can't raise the money that way. If we can't do it that way, then come back to me and we'll talk about it." You know what happened? When you appeal to God's people, let them know what the needs are, God's people meet the need. You don't have to cheapen the gospel by appealing to the lost world for money. What we take to a lost world is Jesus. We are not selling merchandise. We are giving them something. So John says it is the responsibility of Christian believers to support the work of the Lord.

Third, when we receive Christian workers (v. 8) and have a part in their ministry (the word receive really means to underwrite, to foot the bill), we become "fellowhelpers to the truth." Some of you, down in your heart of hearts, would like to have preached the gospel. Some of you would like to have gone to the missionfield, but it didn't work out. It just wasn't God's way.

Now, as you give and help others, you become a fellow helper of the truth. You share in the ministry.

I got excited when Brother Webster Carroll was here visiting our church en route back to Uganda. He's been there as a missionary for many years. He was talking about winning people to Jesus over there, organizing teams, teaching them to play basketball, and then giving testimonies for the Lord. Through the ministry of that man I can have a part, I can be a fellow helper, in winning people to Jesus in Uganda. I expect when I get to heaven to have some people from Africa walk up to me and say, "I want to thank you." I will look at them puzzled and say, "What for?" "You had a part in my salvation. Your gift sent a missionary who told me about Jesus."

John says to Gaius, You are well beloved, a commendable Christian. I want to be the kind of Christian who's a blessing, don't you?

I have a list of evangelists and Bible teachers for whom I pray every morning. I even have the itinerary of some of them, so I know where they are every week. I want to be that kind of Christian too—a man of prayer.

II. DIOTREPHES: A CANTANKEROUS CHRISTIAN

Who was Diotrephes? The name occurs everywhere in secular Greek literature. It is identified with Greek aristocracy, even nobility. Evidently this man was upper class, among the elite, when he came to the Lord. He was accustomed to being in the spotlight. He was trying to run the church.

Have you ever met such a person? I go to revival meetings, go into a church, and can be there not two services, but if one of those types is there I can spot him. I was in a revival meeting a few years ago. The first night after the service I was shaking hands with people, and when a man came by, it was just like electricity when he shook my hand. Later I asked the pastor, "Who is that guy?" "Oh, that's Brother So-and-So. He's the head deacon." I said, "You are going to have trouble with him." He said, "Oh, no, you don't understand, he's the most important member of our church." A few months later that pastor called me and said, "You were exactly right." He said that man gave him more trouble. Talk about a troublemaker. You couldn't get along with him. He had to be first in everything. Number one. Run this, tell everybody to do that. He was running the show.

The work of the Lord is hindered, the church of Jesus Christ is kept from being what it ought to be in many a local situation, because some Diotrephes is so filled with pride, so filled with himself, that he wants to be top dog all the time.

Colossians 1:18 says that Christ is the one who is supposed to have preeminence. Why does God bless First Baptist Church of Jacksonville? Jesus is the one who gets the preeminence around here. He's number one. There are no big shots—or little shots— around here.

How does a Diotrephes get into a church? He slides in, and if a church is not led by deeply spiritual individuals, he may wiggle into a key place of leadership. Once he gets in, he begins to throw his weight around. This Diotrephes wouldn't accept even the authority of John. John says, "I wrote unto the church, but Diotrephes . . ." (v. 9).

Diotrephes went around the church with "prating" words. The root of that word means to bubble up, like an air bubble or a water bubble. A water bubble is just water around nothing, an empty bubble. Diotrephes was a gossip, blabbing malicious words. Then John says, "Neither does he receive the brethren." In other words, these traveling preachers would come through, but Diotrephes was so insecure that he couldn't stand the ministry of other men. In fact, if anybody else tried to receive them, he wanted to kick *them* out of the church.

Don't be a Diotrephes. Don't have to be first. If I can't be president of my class, I won't come. If they don't elect me chairperson, I won't be on the committee at all. If I can't play first base, I won't play on the team. It reminds me of a boy I knew back home. We were real poor. We had only one football on the whole block, and this boy owned it. The problem was, because he owned the football, he wanted to set up all the rules. When you didn't like his rules, he would just pick up his football and go home. That kind of person can make life miserable. A little power in the heart and life of a prideful Christian is a dangerous thing.

III. DEMETRIUS: A CONSISTENT CHRISTIAN

"Demetrius hath good report of all men" (v. 12). The lost world spoke well of Demetrius. ". . . And of the truth itself." You could take the word of God, put it next to the life of Demetrius, and he was consistent.

That's the kind of Christian you and I must want to be—one who helps people walk in the truth and live the truth and love the truth. Jesus is the one who helps us be that kind of Christian. He is the only one who can change our life and make it of "good report."

Conclusion

JOHN'S EPISTLES ARE ENDED. HIS FIRST LETTER EMPHASIZES THE CERTAINTY that believers have in Christ. Repeatedly he says we can know. What a contrast that is to speculations of non-Christian philosophies. Our Savior is "the truth" (John 14:6).

Second and third John touch the Christian life in beautiful, practical ways. These postscripts to John's first letter underscore emphases already introduced. The teaching in them is not new. Rather, truth stated in 1 John is illustrated in 2 and 3 John.

Second John provides an added emphasis on the dangers of anti-Christian teaching. Here we find how the believer is to confront and conquer aberrant teaching. Third John climaxes the trilogy. Second John is directed to a woman; third John addresses a man. Second John urges a strong response to false teaching; third John counsels against undue harshness.

The brevity of these letters should not cause us to be brief in our contemplation of their messages. We should never measure the message of a book by its length. The Holy Spirit never multiplies words to convey his message.

I can almost imagine John, the loving pastor, laying down his pen. Perhaps he did not know that the Holy Spirit would open up heaven to him and allow him to write of things past, present, and yet to come (Revelation 1:19). So in these little letters the aged pastor writes with all the fervor of his soul to encourage God's people to intellectual certainty, doctrinal purity, and practical charity.